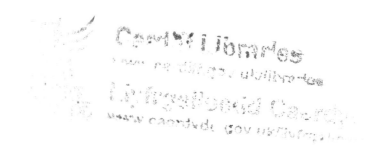

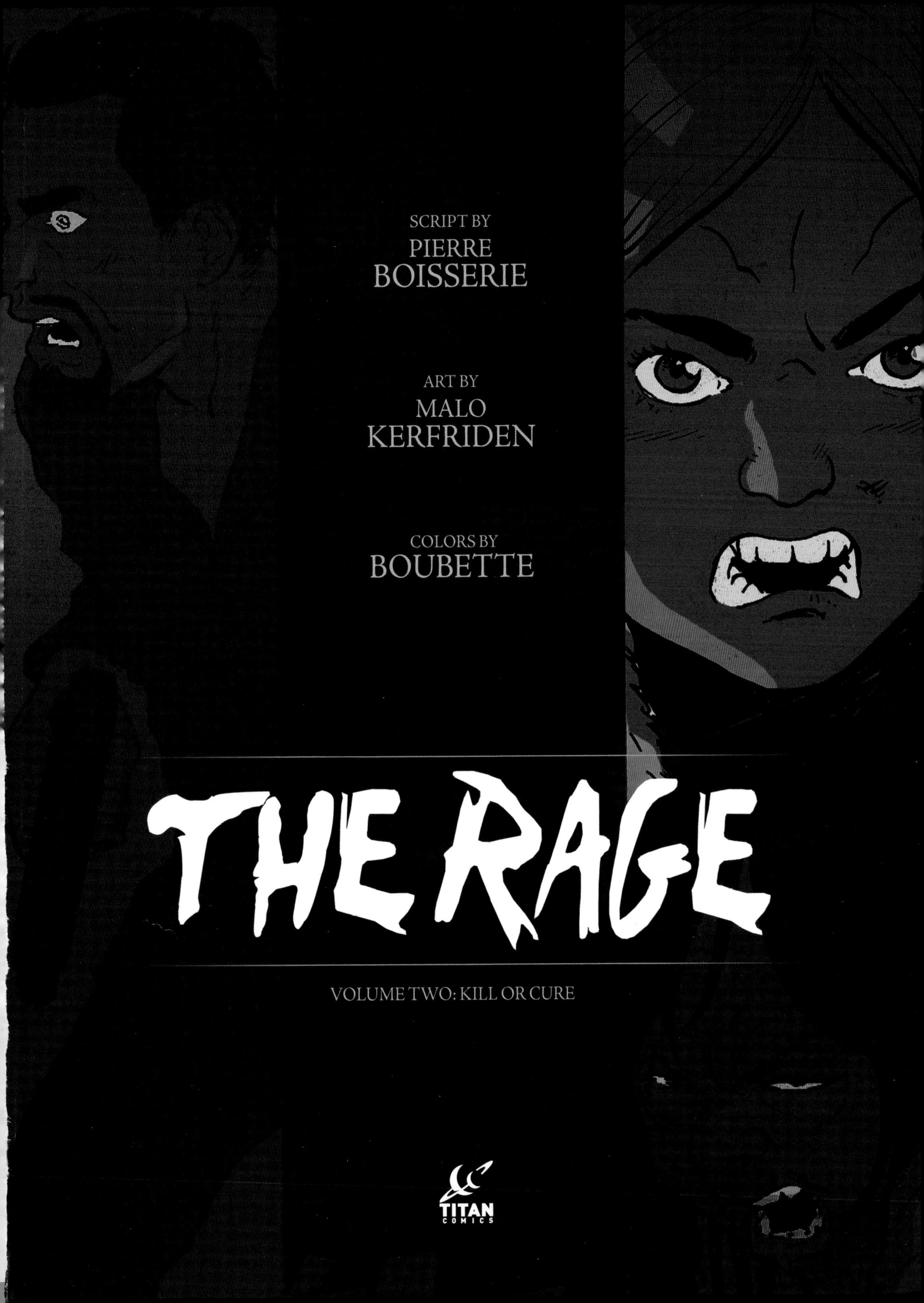

SCRIPT BY
PIERRE
BOISSERIE

ART BY
MALO
KERFRIDEN

COLORS BY
BOUBETTE

THE RAGE

VOLUME TWO: KILL OR CURE

TITAN COMICS

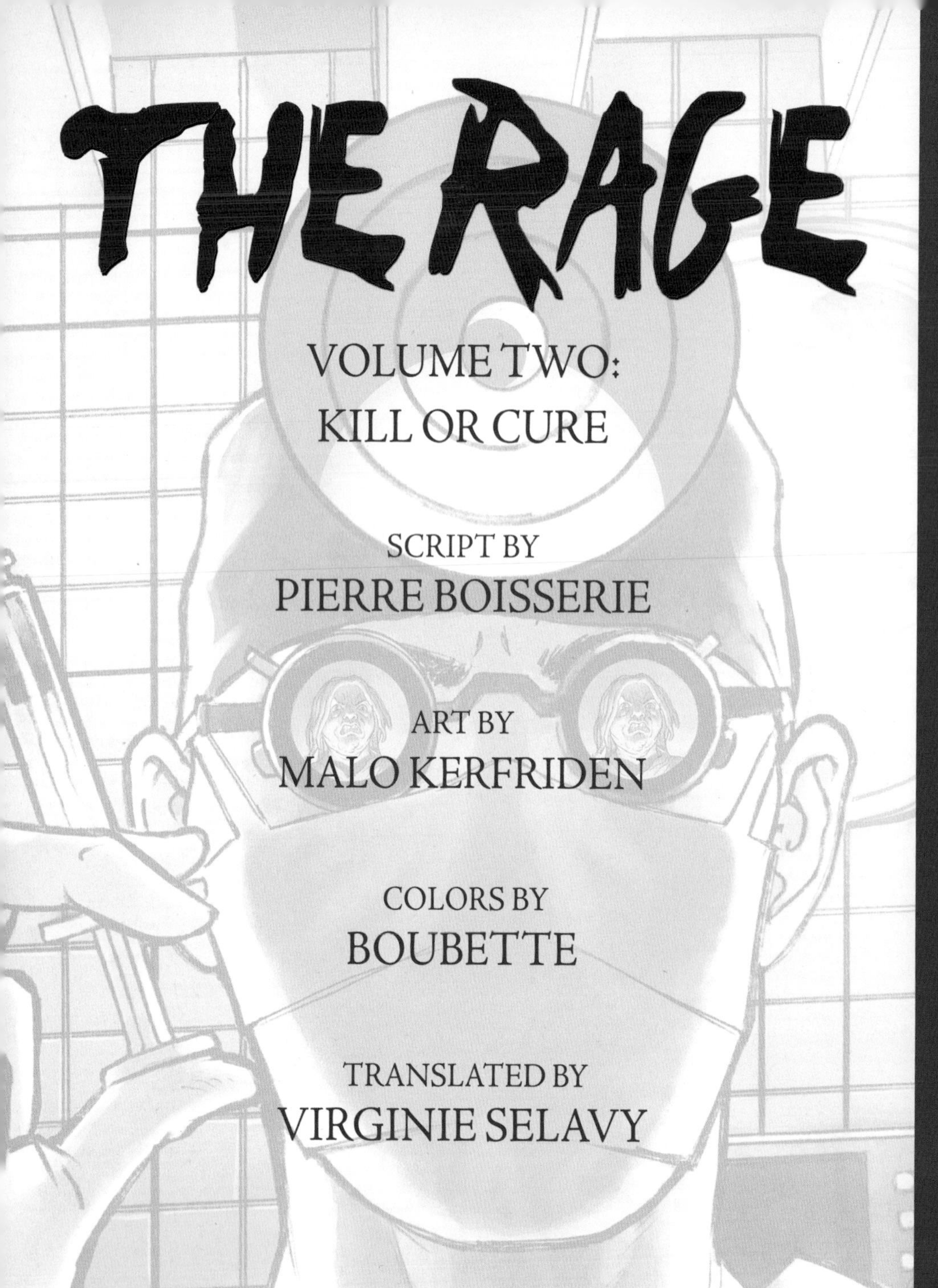

THE RAGE

VOLUME TWO: KILL OR CURE

SCRIPT BY
PIERRE BOISSERIE

ART BY
MALO KERFRIDEN

COLORS BY
BOUBETTE

TRANSLATED BY
VIRGINIE SELAVY

What did you think of this book? We love to hear from our readers.
Please email us at: readercomments@titanemail.com,
or write to us at the above address.

To receive news, competitions, and exclusive offers online,
please sign up for the Titan Comics newsletter on our website:
www.titan-comics.com

Follow us on Twitter @ComicsTitan

Visit us at facebook.com/comicstitan

TITAN COMICS

COLLECTION EDITOR
Gabriela Houston
COLLECTION DESIGNER
Donna Askem
SENIOR EDITOR
Steve White
TITAN COMICS EDITORIAL
Andrew James, Tom Williams
PRODUCTION SUPERVISOR
Jackie Flook
PRODUCTION ASSISTANT
Peter James
PRODUCTION MANAGER
Obi Onuora
STUDIO MANAGER
Emma Smith
CIRCULATION MANAGER
Steve Tothill
MARKETING MANAGER
Ricky Claydon
SENIOR MARKETING
AND PRESS EXECUTIVE
Owen Johnson
PUBLISHING MANAGER
Darryl Tothill
PUBLISHING DIRECTOR
Chris Teather
OPERATIONS DIRECTOR
Leigh Baulch
EXECUTIVE DIRECTOR
Vivian Cheung
PUBLISHER
Nick Landau

The Rage: Kill or Cure

ISBN: 9781782760887

Published by Titan Comics
A division of Titan Publishing Group Ltd.
144 Southwark St.
London
SE1 0UP

A CIP catalogue record for this title is available from the British Library.

First edition: February 2015

Originally published in 2013 by 12 BIS, France as *La Rage: Fred*

10 9 8 7 6 5 4 3 2 1

Printed in China.
Titan Comics. TC0199

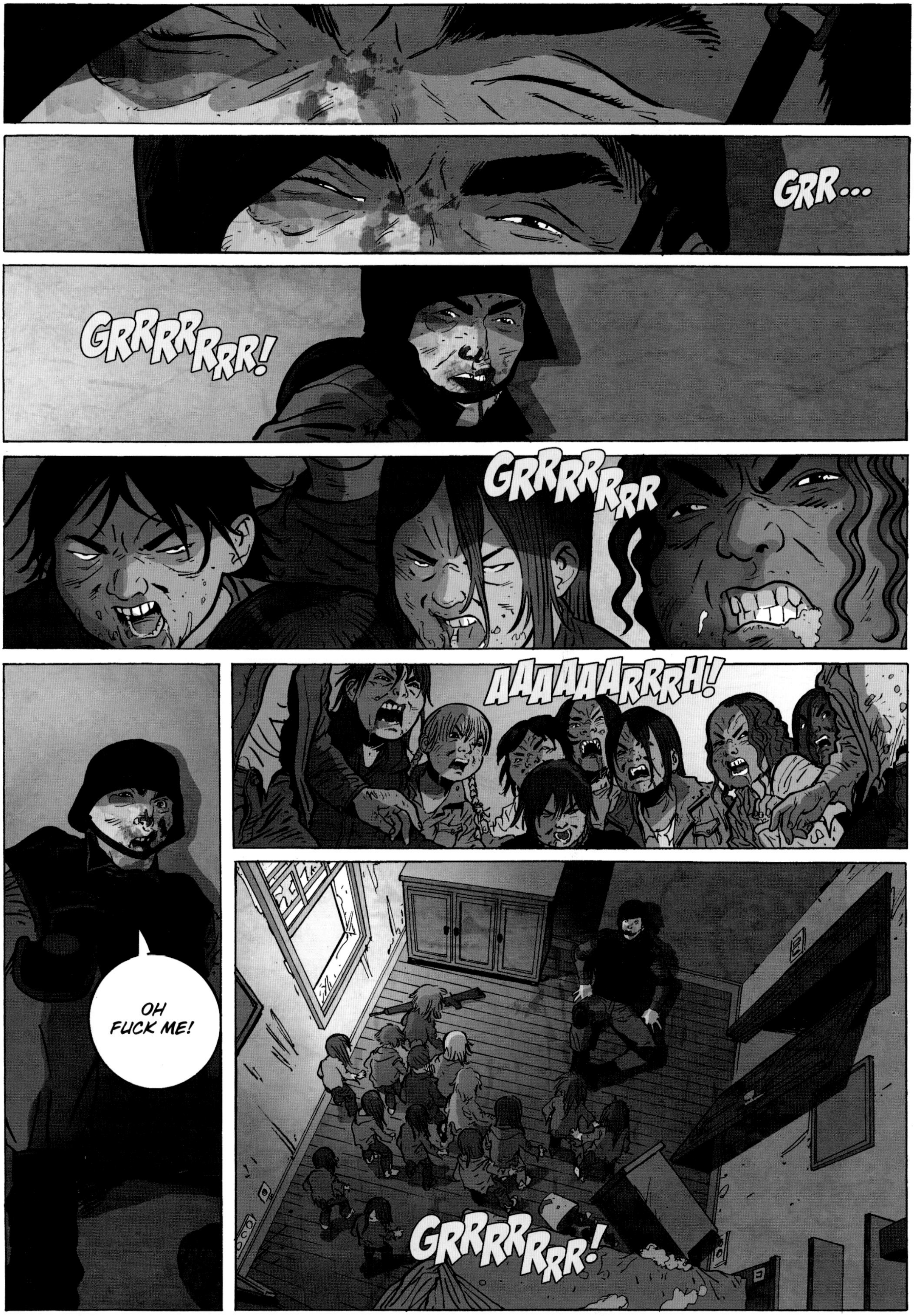
GRR...
GRRRRRRR!
GRRRRRRR
AAAAAARRRH!
OH FUCK ME!
GRRRRRRR!

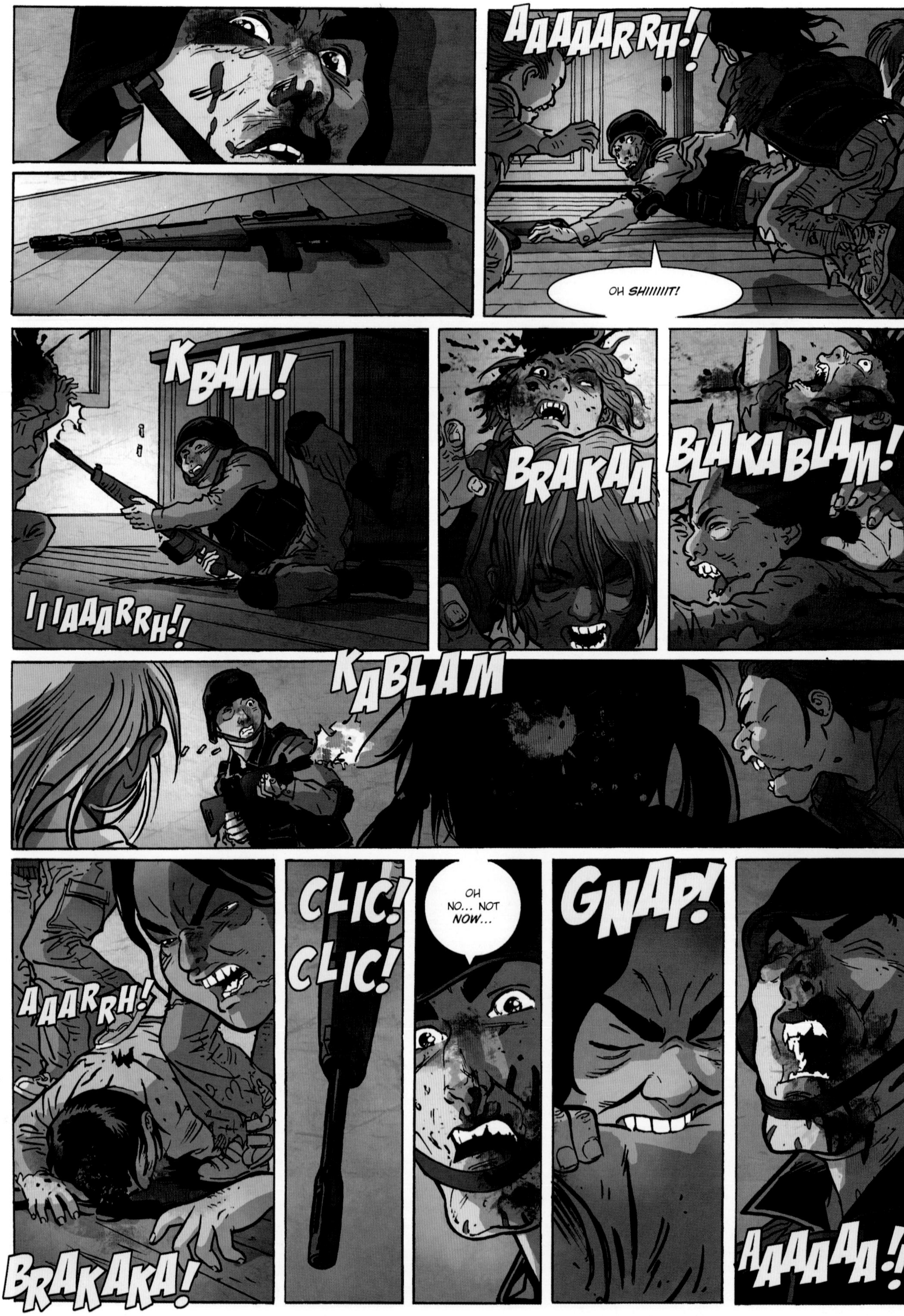
AAAAARRH!!
OH SHIIIIIIT!
KBAM!
IIIAAARRH!!
BRAKAA
BLAKABLAM!
KABLAM
AAARRH!
BRAKAKA!
CLIC! CLIC!
OH NO... NOT NOW...
GNAP!
AAAAAA!!

GET **OFF**, YOU LITTLE **SHIT!**

AAAAARR!

KRASH!

AAAAARR!!

KRAK!

IIIAARR!

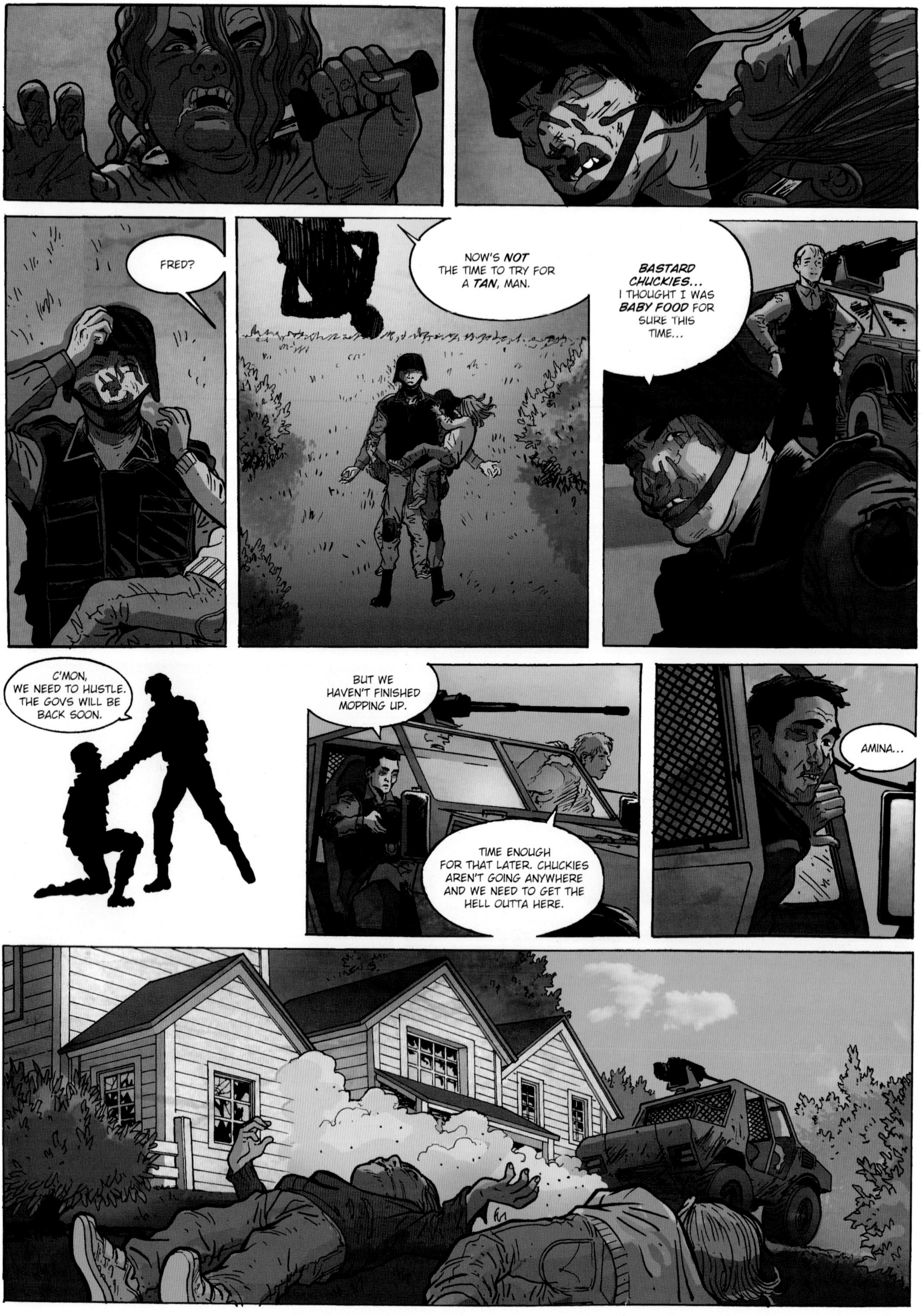
FRED?
NOW'S NOT THE TIME TO TRY FOR A TAN, MAN.
BASTARD CHUCKIES... I THOUGHT I WAS BABY FOOD FOR SURE THIS TIME...
C'MON, WE NEED TO HUSTLE. THE GOVS WILL BE BACK SOON.
BUT WE HAVEN'T FINISHED MOPPING UP.
TIME ENOUGH FOR THAT LATER. CHUCKIES AREN'T GOING ANYWHERE AND WE NEED TO GET THE HELL OUTTA HERE.
AMINA...

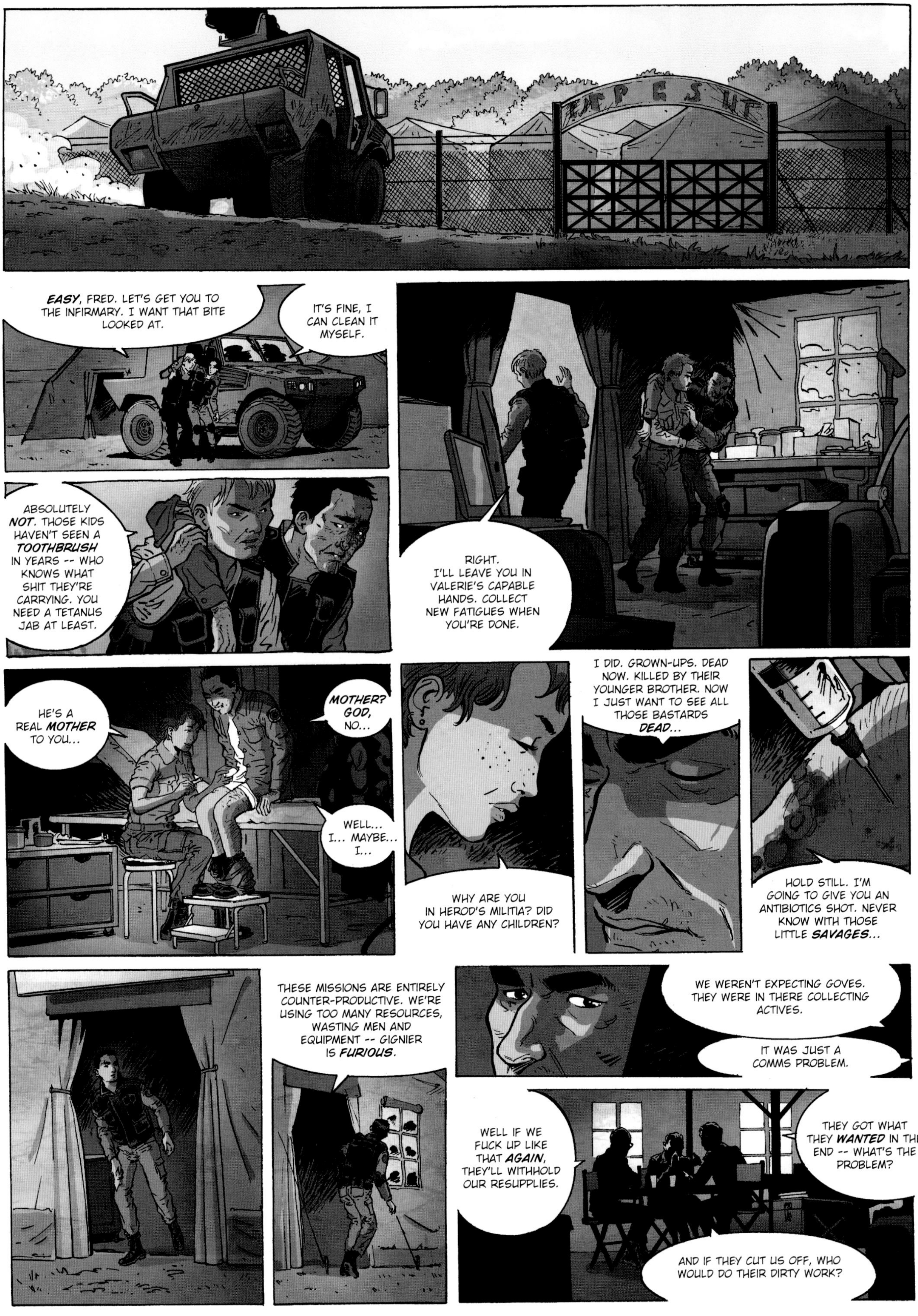
EASY, FRED. LET'S GET YOU TO THE INFIRMARY. I WANT THAT BITE LOOKED AT.
IT'S FINE, I CAN CLEAN IT MYSELF.
ABSOLUTELY NOT. THOSE KIDS HAVEN'T SEEN A TOOTHBRUSH IN YEARS -- WHO KNOWS WHAT SHIT THEY'RE CARRYING. YOU NEED A TETANUS JAB AT LEAST.
RIGHT. I'LL LEAVE YOU IN VALERIE'S CAPABLE HANDS. COLLECT NEW FATIGUES WHEN YOU'RE DONE.
HE'S A REAL MOTHER TO YOU...
MOTHER? GOD, NO...
WELL... I... MAYBE... I...
WHY ARE YOU IN HEROD'S MILITIA? DID YOU HAVE ANY CHILDREN?
I DID. GROWN-UPS. DEAD NOW. KILLED BY THEIR YOUNGER BROTHER. NOW I JUST WANT TO SEE ALL THOSE BASTARDS DEAD...
HOLD STILL. I'M GOING TO GIVE YOU AN ANTIBIOTICS SHOT. NEVER KNOW WITH THOSE LITTLE SAVAGES...
THESE MISSIONS ARE ENTIRELY COUNTER-PRODUCTIVE. WE'RE USING TOO MANY RESOURCES, WASTING MEN AND EQUIPMENT -- GIGNIER IS FURIOUS.
WE WEREN'T EXPECTING GOVES. THEY WERE IN THERE COLLECTING ACTIVES.
IT WAS JUST A COMMS PROBLEM.
WELL IF WE FUCK UP LIKE THAT AGAIN, THEY'LL WITHHOLD OUR RESUPPLIES.
THEY GOT WHAT THEY WANTED IN THE END -- WHAT'S THE PROBLEM?
AND IF THEY CUT US OFF, WHO WOULD DO THEIR DIRTY WORK?

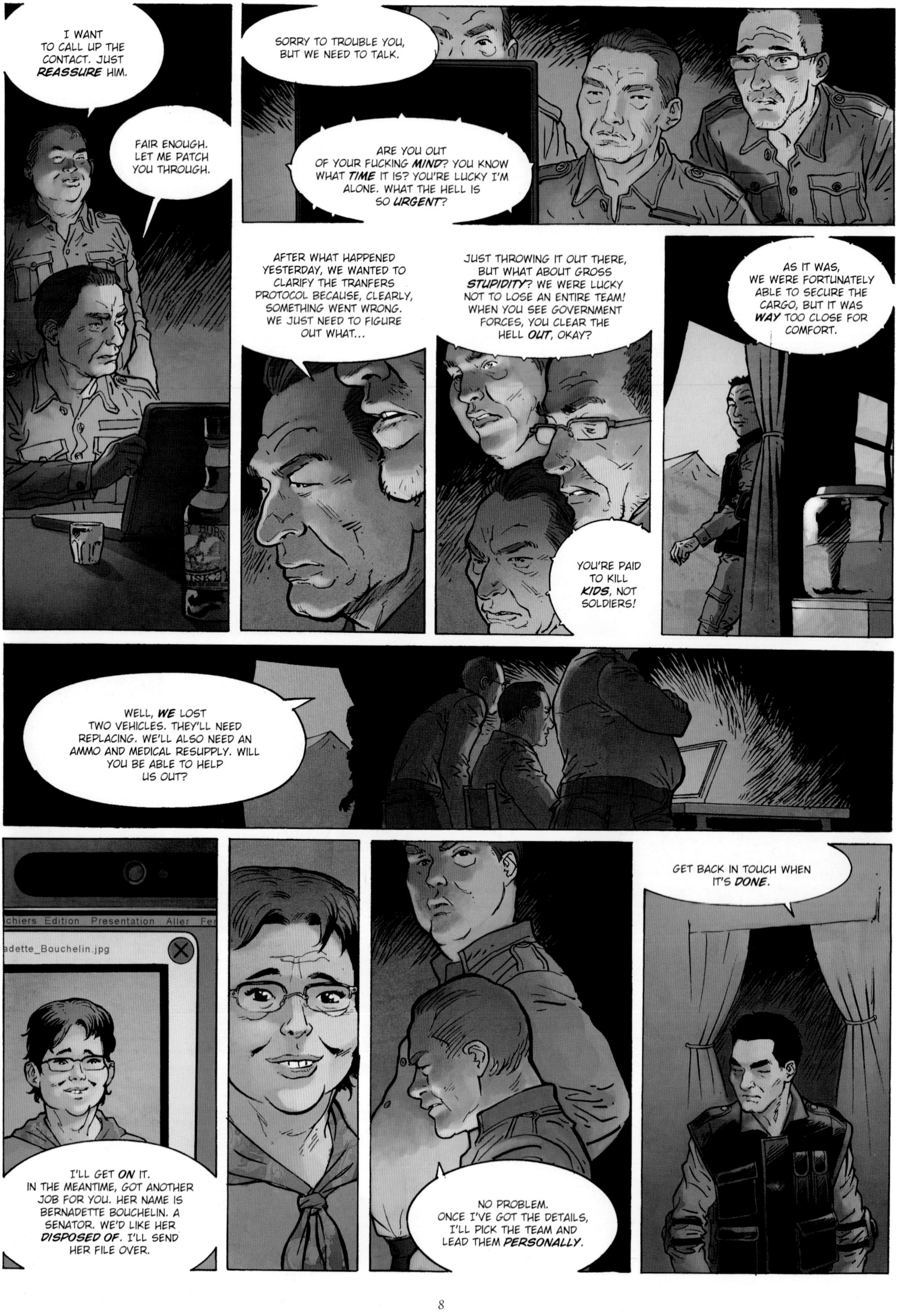
I WANT TO CALL UP THE CONTACT. JUST REASSURE HIM.
FAIR ENOUGH. LET ME PATCH YOU THROUGH.
SORRY TO TROUBLE YOU, BUT WE NEED TO TALK.
ARE YOU OUT OF YOUR FUCKING MIND? YOU KNOW WHAT TIME IT IS? YOU'RE LUCKY I'M ALONE. WHAT THE HELL IS SO URGENT?
AFTER WHAT HAPPENED YESTERDAY, WE WANTED TO CLARIFY THE TRANFERS PROTOCOL BECAUSE, CLEARLY, SOMETHING WENT WRONG. WE JUST NEED TO FIGURE OUT WHAT...
JUST THROWING IT OUT THERE, BUT WHAT ABOUT GROSS STUPIDITY? WE WERE LUCKY NOT TO LOSE AN ENTIRE TEAM! WHEN YOU SEE GOVERNMENT FORCES, YOU CLEAR THE HELL OUT, OKAY?
YOU'RE PAID TO KILL KIDS, NOT SOLDIERS!
AS IT WAS, WE WERE FORTUNATELY ABLE TO SECURE THE CARGO, BUT IT WAS WAY TOO CLOSE FOR COMFORT.
WELL, WE LOST TWO VEHICLES. THEY'LL NEED REPLACING. WE'LL ALSO NEED AN AMMO AND MEDICAL RESUPPLY. WILL YOU BE ABLE TO HELP US OUT?
chiers Edition Presentation Aller Fe
adette_Bouchelin.jpg
I'LL GET ON IT. IN THE MEANTIME, GOT ANOTHER JOB FOR YOU. HER NAME IS BERNADETTE BOUCHELIN. A SENATOR. WE'D LIKE HER DISPOSED OF. I'LL SEND HER FILE OVER.
NO PROBLEM. ONCE I'VE GOT THE DETAILS, I'LL PICK THE TEAM AND LEAD THEM PERSONALLY.
GET BACK IN TOUCH WHEN IT'S DONE.

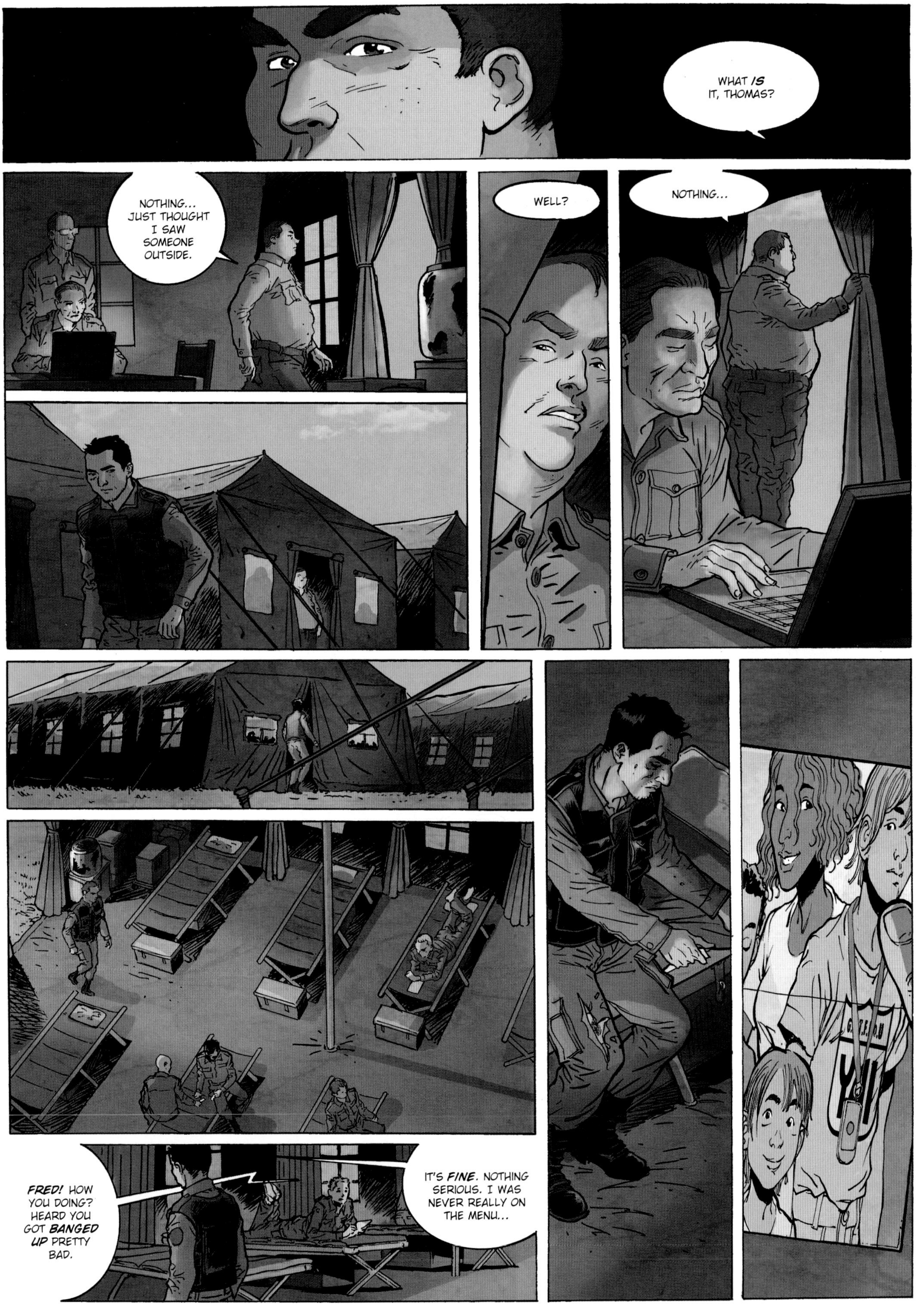
WHAT *IS* IT, THOMAS?
NOTHING... JUST THOUGHT I SAW SOMEONE OUTSIDE.
WELL?
NOTHING...
FRED! HOW YOU DOING? HEARD YOU GOT *BANGED UP* PRETTY BAD.
IT'S *FINE*. NOTHING SERIOUS. I WAS NEVER REALLY ON THE MENU...

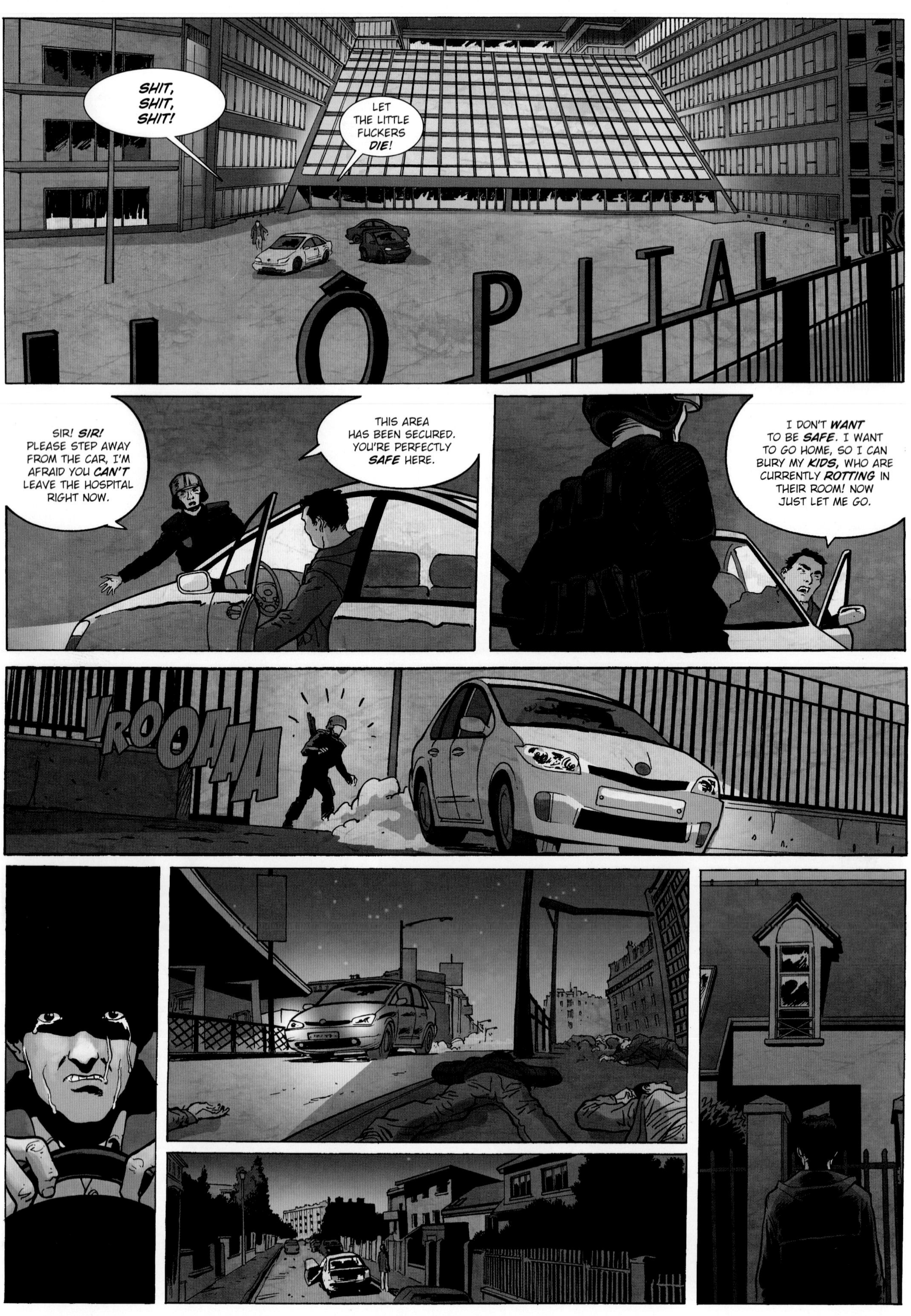
SHIT, SHIT, SHIT!
LET THE LITTLE FUCKERS DIE!
HÔPITAL EURO
SIR! SIR! PLEASE STEP AWAY FROM THE CAR, I'M AFRAID YOU CAN'T LEAVE THE HOSPITAL RIGHT NOW.
THIS AREA HAS BEEN SECURED. YOU'RE PERFECTLY SAFE HERE.
I DON'T WANT TO BE SAFE. I WANT TO GO HOME, SO I CAN BURY MY KIDS, WHO ARE CURRENTLY ROTTING IN THEIR ROOM! NOW JUST LET ME GO.
VROOAAA

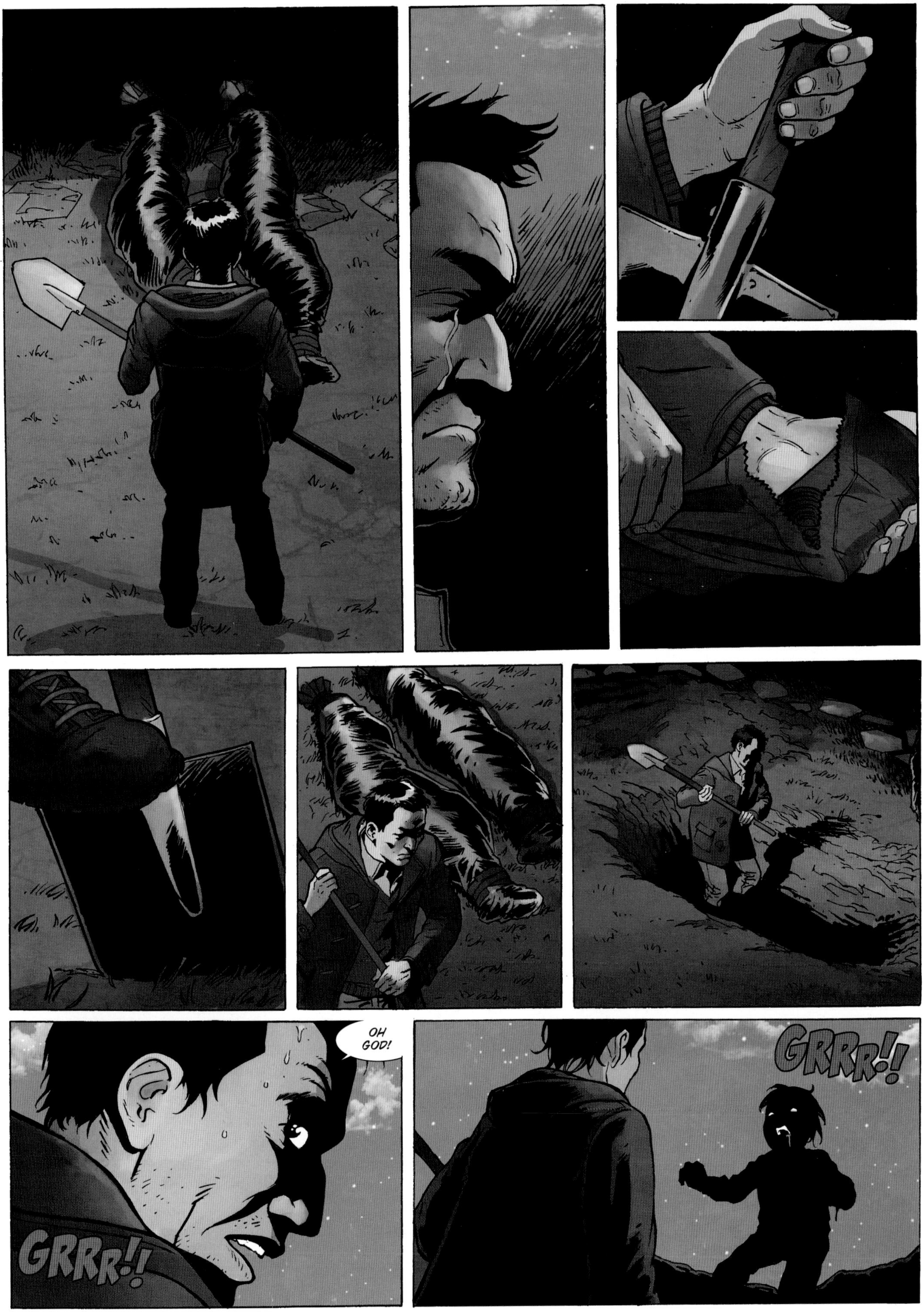
OH GOD!
GRRR!!
GRRR!!

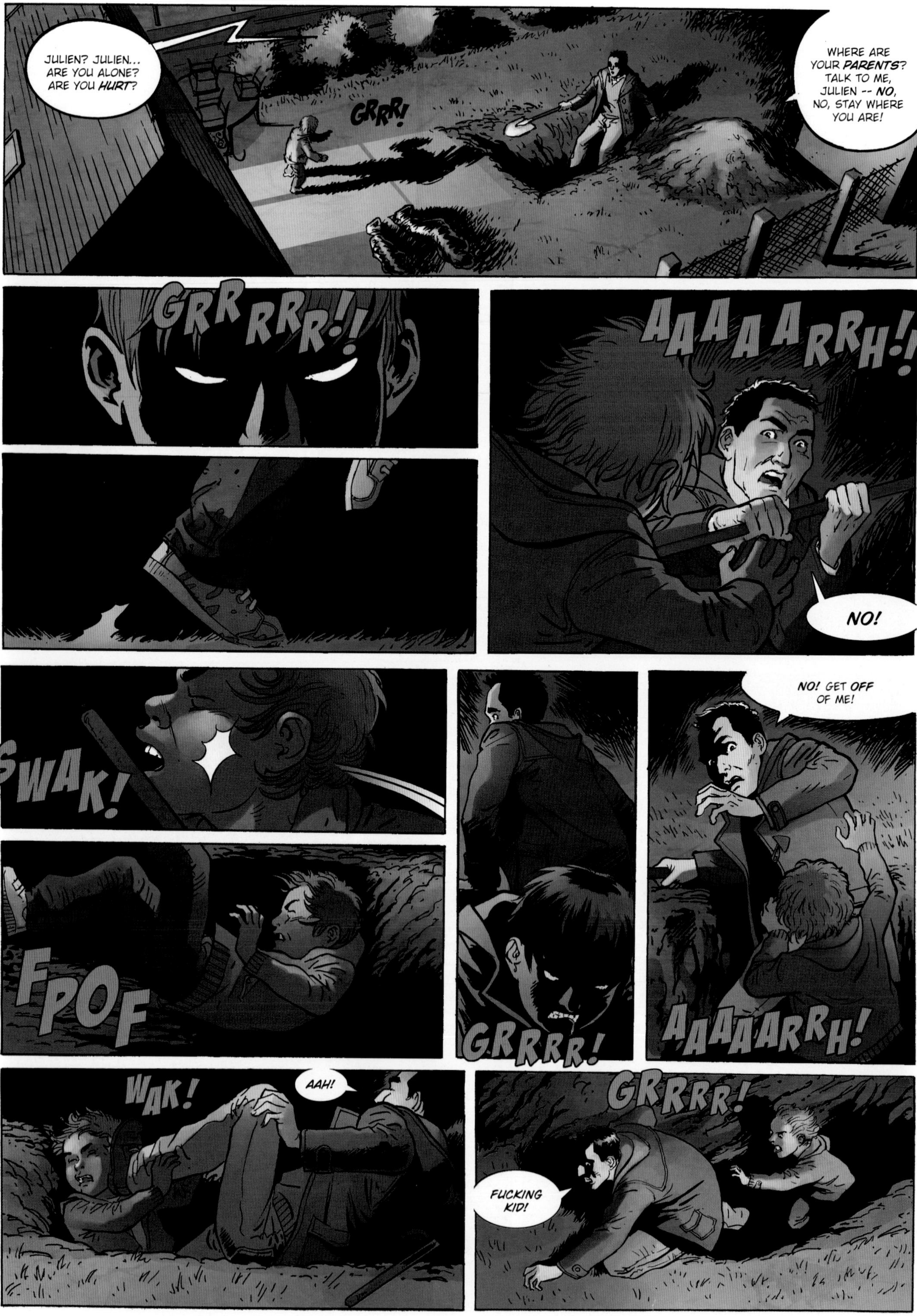
JULIEN? JULIEN... ARE YOU ALONE? ARE YOU HURT?
GRRR!
WHERE ARE YOUR PARENTS? TALK TO ME, JULIEN -- NO, NO, STAY WHERE YOU ARE!
GRRRRR!!
AAAAARRH!!
NO!
SWAK!
FPOF
NO! GET OFF OF ME!
GRRRR!
AAAAARRH!
WAK!
AAH!
GRRRR!
FUCKING KID!

FUCKING MONSTER CHILD!

WAK!

HAD *ENOUGH?*
-≥HNN≤- WANT...
WANT *MORE?*

GRRR!!

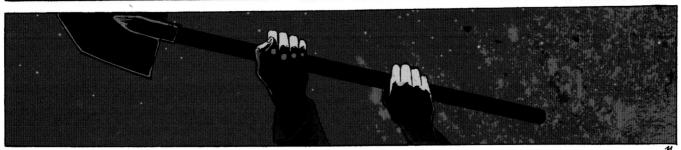

WAK!

WAK!

WAK!

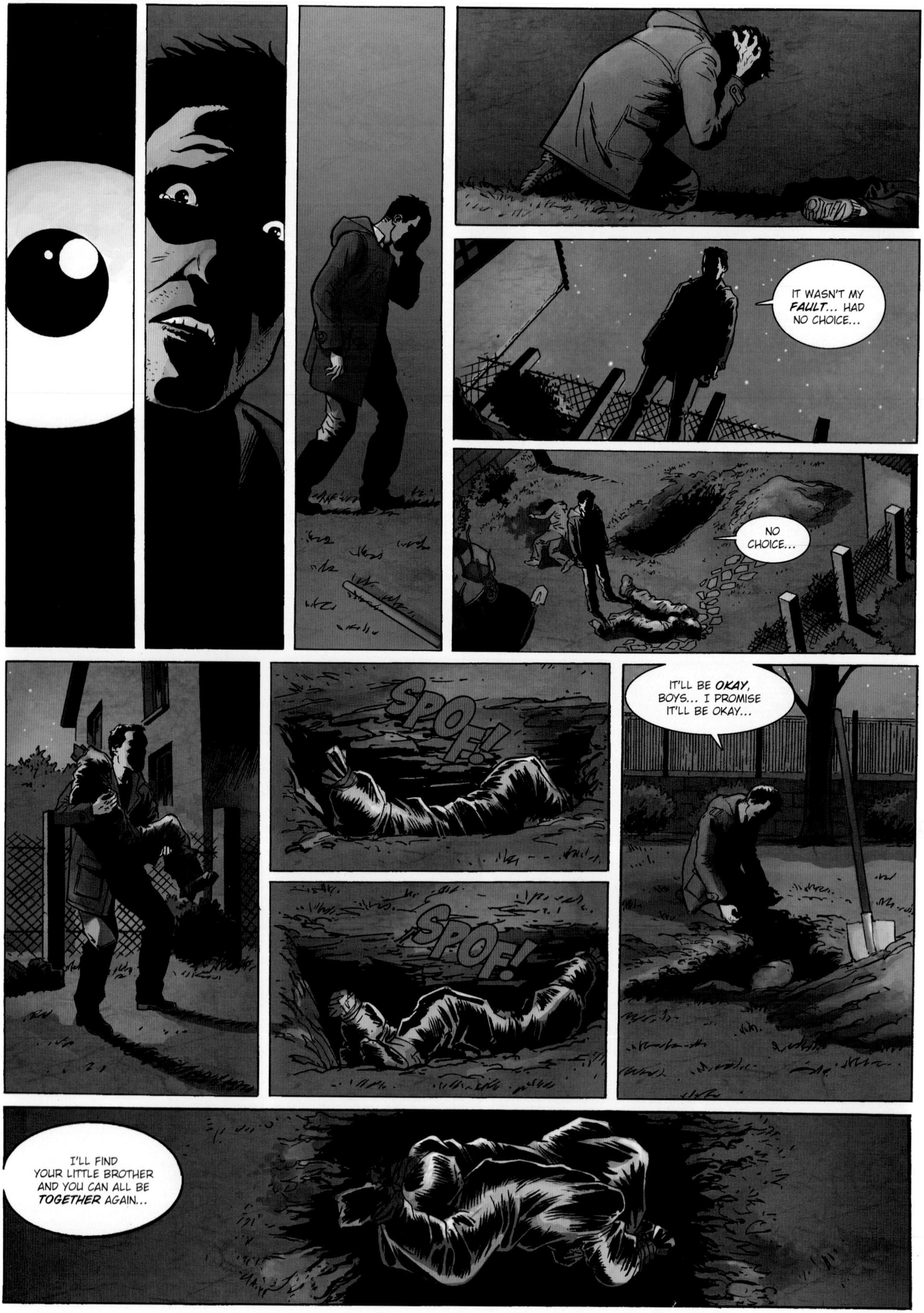
IT WASN'T MY FAULT... HAD NO CHOICE...
NO CHOICE...
SPOF!
SPOF!
IT'LL BE OKAY, BOYS... I PROMISE IT'LL BE OKAY...
I'LL FIND YOUR LITTLE BROTHER AND YOU CAN ALL BE TOGETHER AGAIN...

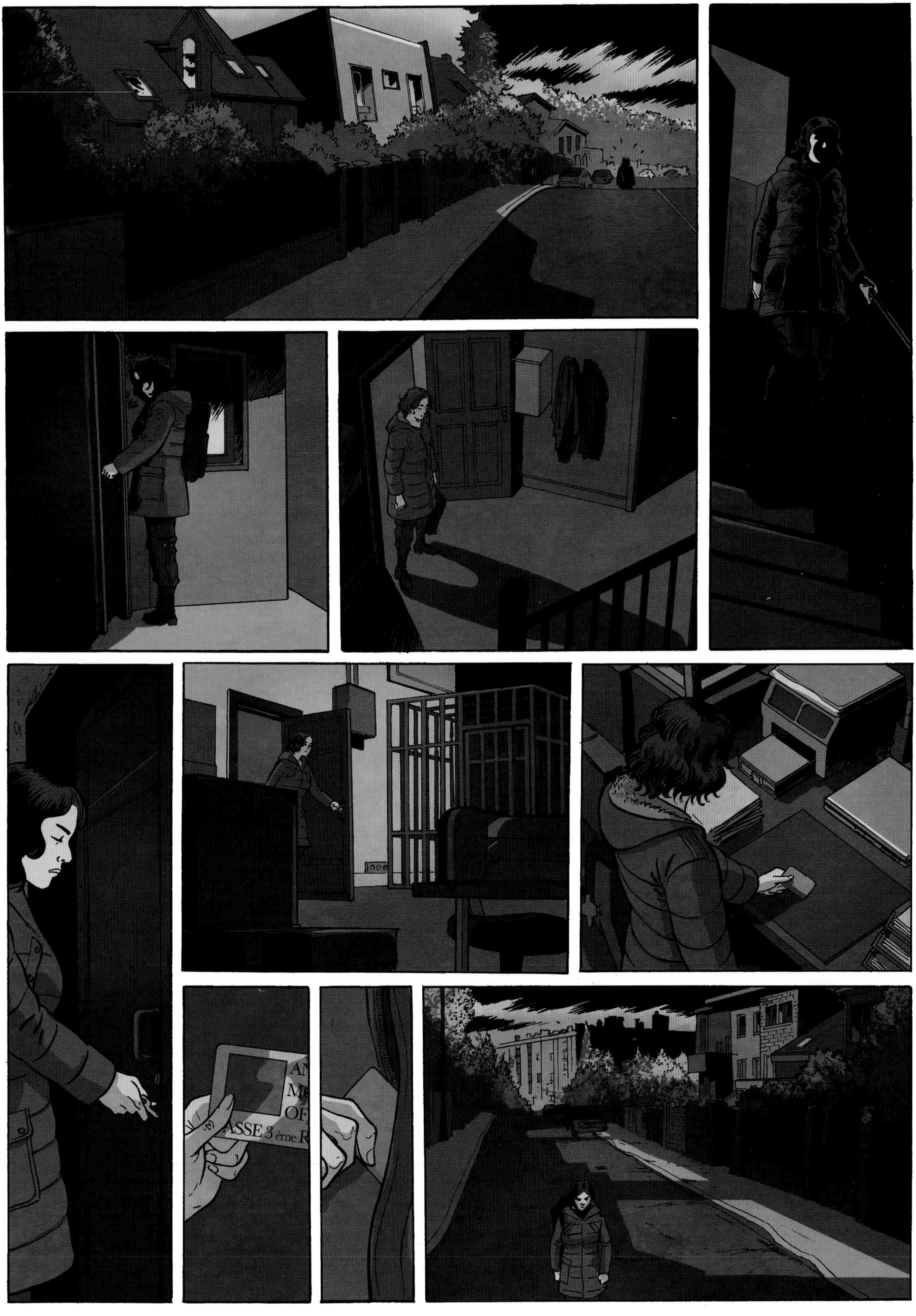
AN
ME
OF
ASSE 3 ème R

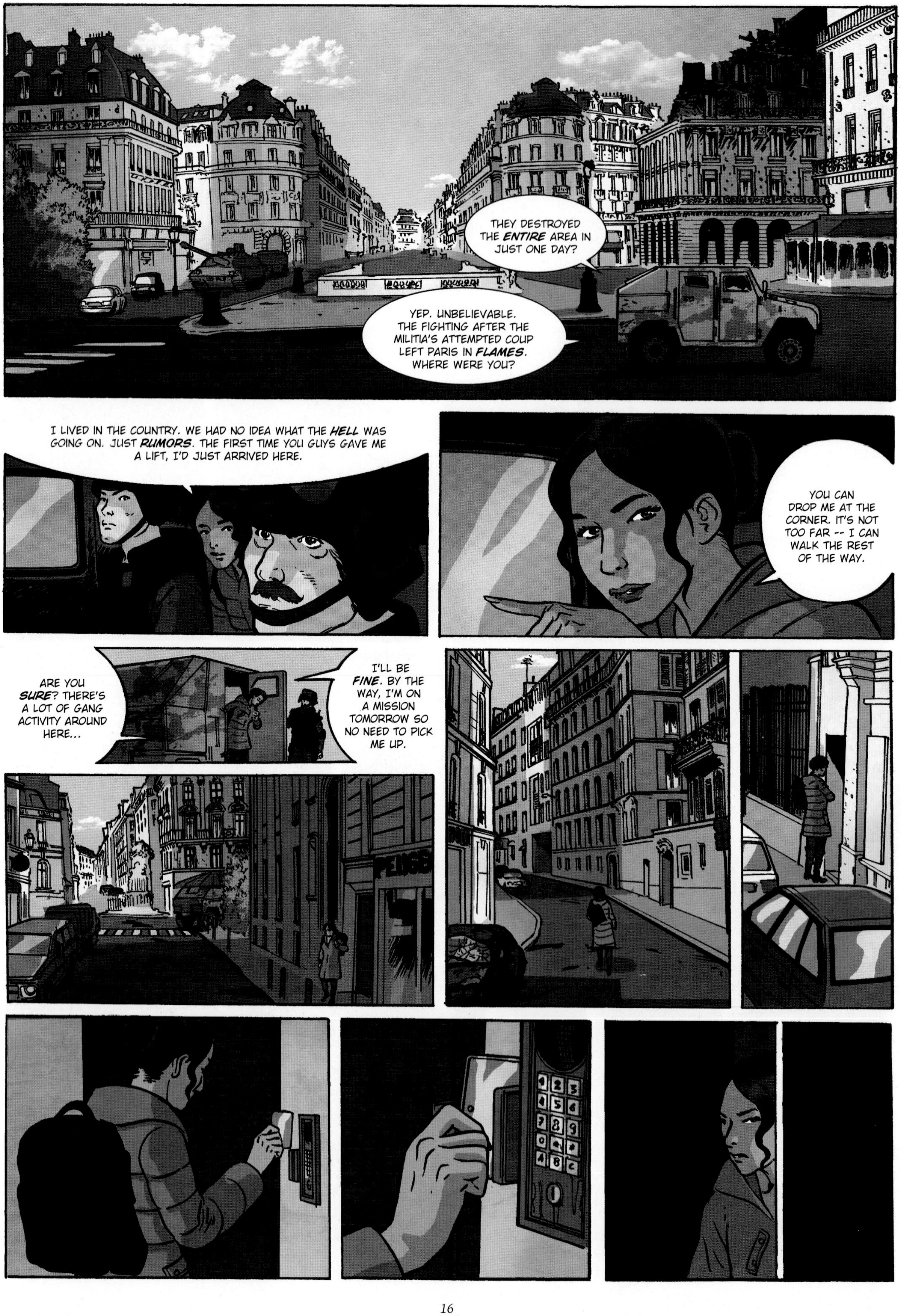
THEY DESTROYED THE ENTIRE AREA IN JUST ONE DAY?
YEP. UNBELIEVABLE. THE FIGHTING AFTER THE MILITIA'S ATTEMPTED COUP LEFT PARIS IN FLAMES. WHERE WERE YOU?
I LIVED IN THE COUNTRY. WE HAD NO IDEA WHAT THE HELL WAS GOING ON. JUST RUMORS. THE FIRST TIME YOU GUYS GAVE ME A LIFT, I'D JUST ARRIVED HERE.
YOU CAN DROP ME AT THE CORNER. IT'S NOT TOO FAR -- I CAN WALK THE REST OF THE WAY.
ARE YOU SURE? THERE'S A LOT OF GANG ACTIVITY AROUND HERE...
I'LL BE FINE. BY THE WAY, I'M ON A MISSION TOMORROW SO NO NEED TO PICK ME UP.

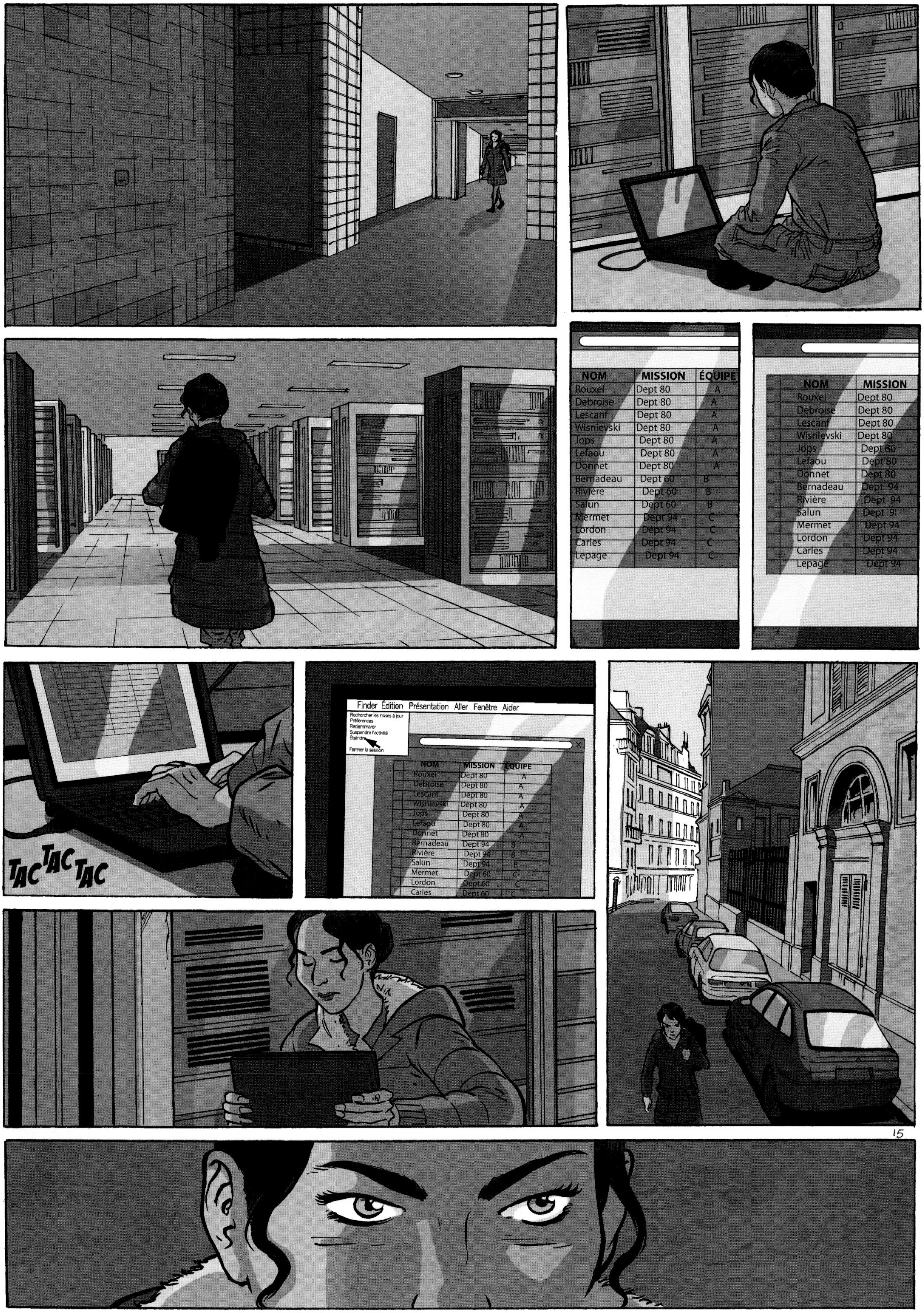
NOM MISSION ÉQUIPE
Rouxel Dept 80 A
Debroise Dept 80 A
Lescanf Dept 80 A
Wisnievski Dept 80 A
Jops Dept 80 A
Lefaou Dept 80 A
Donnet Dept 80 A
Bernadeau Dept 60 B
Rivière Dept 60 B
Salun Dept 60 B
Mermet Dept 94 C
Lordon Dept 94 C
Carles Dept 94 C
Lepage Dept 94 C
NOM MISSION
Rouxel Dept 80
Debroise Dept 80
Lescanf Dept 80
Wisnievski Dept 80
Jops Dept 80
Lefaou Dept 80
Donnet Dept 80
Bernadeau Dept 94
Rivière Dept 94
Salun Dept 9l
Mermet Dept 94
Lordon Dept 94
Carles Dept 94
Lepage Dept 94
TAC TAC TAC
Finder Édition Présentation Aller Fenêtre Aider
Rechercher les mises à jour
Préférences
Redemmarer
Suspendre l'activité
Éteindr
Fermer la session
NOM MISSION ÉQUIPE
Rouxel Dept 80 A
Debroise Dept 80 A
Lescanf Dept 80 A
Wisnievski Dept 80 A
Jops Dept 80 A
Lefaou Dept 80 A
Donnet Dept 80 A
Bernadeau Dept 94 B
Rivière Dept 94 B
Salun Dept 94 B
Mermet Dept 60 C
Lordon Dept 60 C
Carles Dept 60
15

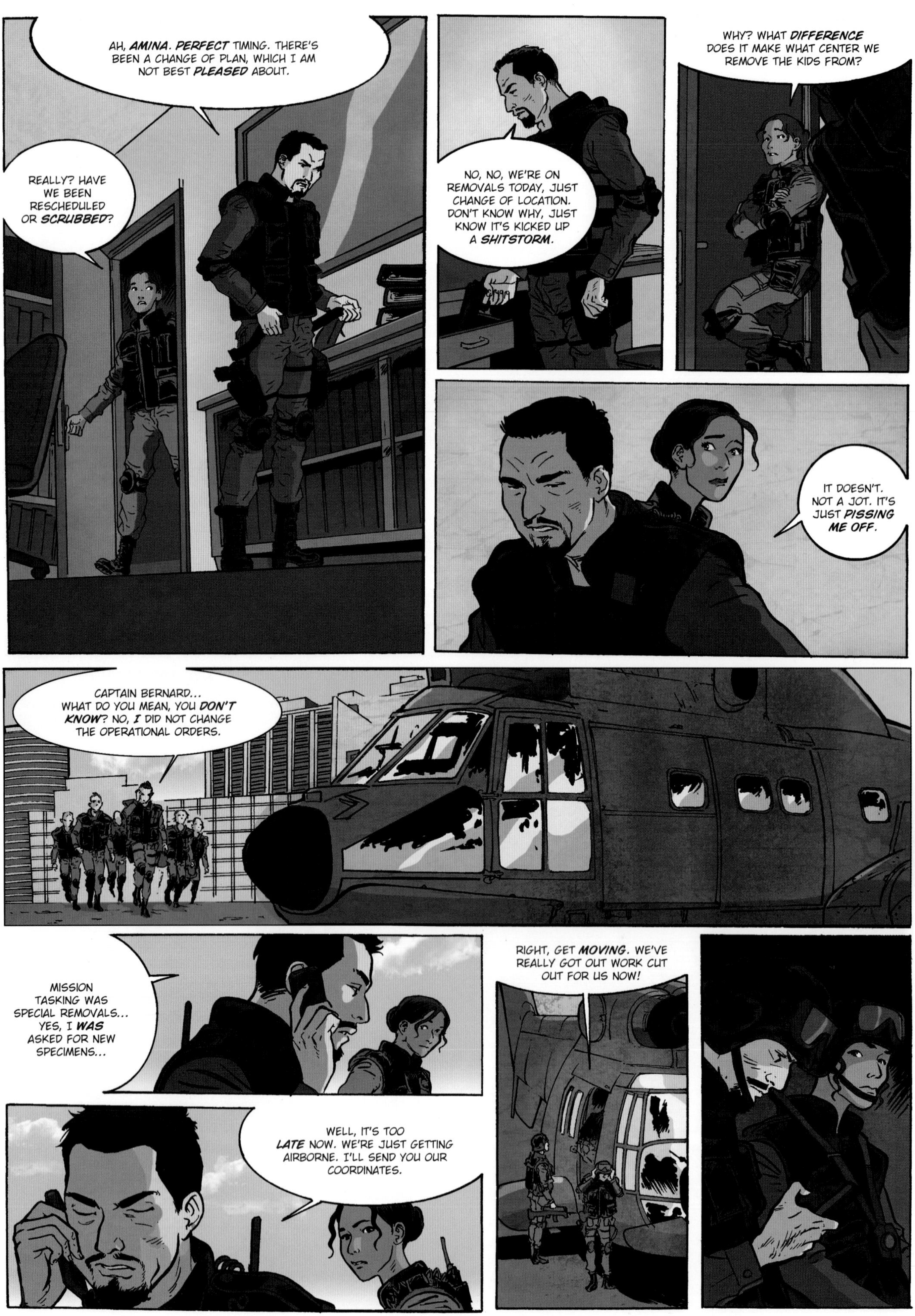
AH, AMINA. PERFECT TIMING. THERE'S BEEN A CHANGE OF PLAN, WHICH I AM NOT BEST PLEASED ABOUT.
REALLY? HAVE WE BEEN RESCHEDULED OR SCRUBBED?
NO, NO, WE'RE ON REMOVALS TODAY, JUST CHANGE OF LOCATION. DON'T KNOW WHY, JUST KNOW IT'S KICKED UP A SHITSTORM.
WHY? WHAT DIFFERENCE DOES IT MAKE WHAT CENTER WE REMOVE THE KIDS FROM?
IT DOESN'T. NOT A JOT. IT'S JUST PISSING ME OFF.
CAPTAIN BERNARD... WHAT DO YOU MEAN, YOU DON'T KNOW? NO, I DID NOT CHANGE THE OPERATIONAL ORDERS.
MISSION TASKING WAS SPECIAL REMOVALS... YES, I WAS ASKED FOR NEW SPECIMENS...
WELL, IT'S TOO LATE NOW. WE'RE JUST GETTING AIRBORNE. I'LL SEND YOU OUR COORDINATES.
RIGHT, GET MOVING. WE'VE REALLY GOT OUT WORK CUT OUT FOR US NOW!

LADIES AND GENTS, L.Z. IN TWO MINUTES. REMOVALS TEAMS ON STANDBY.

VRRRRRRR!

LET'S KEEP THIS FAST AND EFFICIENT. NO DICKING AROUND.

REMEMBER -- THIS HASN'T BEEN AN AMUSEMENT PARK FOR **SOME TIME**, SO PLEASE FOREGO ANY GAMES OF CHUCKIE-BASHING.

CHECK THIS OUT. GOVERNMENT TRUCKS **ALREADY** OUTSIDE THE PARK. WHAT'RE THEY **DOING** HERE?

ALREADY? THAT WAS FAST... FOR A **CHANGE**. I ASKED FOR ANY AVAILABLE LOGISTIC SUPPORT.

VRRRRRRR!

YOU WERE LUCKY. OUR OWN MISSION WAS SCRUBBED AND WE WERE IN THE NEIGHBORHOOD.

HI THERE, MILLER. THANKS FOR GETTING HERE SO QUICKLY. KNOW YOU'VE GOT A LOT ON YOUR PLATE...

WE'VE EVEN HAD TIME TO POSITION SOME ULTRASOUND BUOYS. I KNOW YOU GUYS ONLY HAVE PORTABLES, BUT NOW YOU'LL HAVE THE WHOLE **ZONE** COVERED. SHOULD KEEP YOU SAFE.

ALTHOUGH MY GUYS WILL STAY IN THE REAR WITH THE GEAR.

WHO ARE WE TAKING WITH US?

NOT YOU. YOU'RE **STAYING** WITH LOGISTICS. YOU CAN STABLIZE THE REMOVALS OUT HERE.

BUT I **ALWAYS** GO WITH YOU...

NO PROBLEM, WE'RE FULLY MANNED. ACTIVATE THE DETECTORS, THEN DIVIDE YOUR TEAM INTO GROUPS OF THREE. NO ONE ALONE, **UNDERSTOOD**?

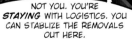

ORDERS ARE YOU **STAY**.

19

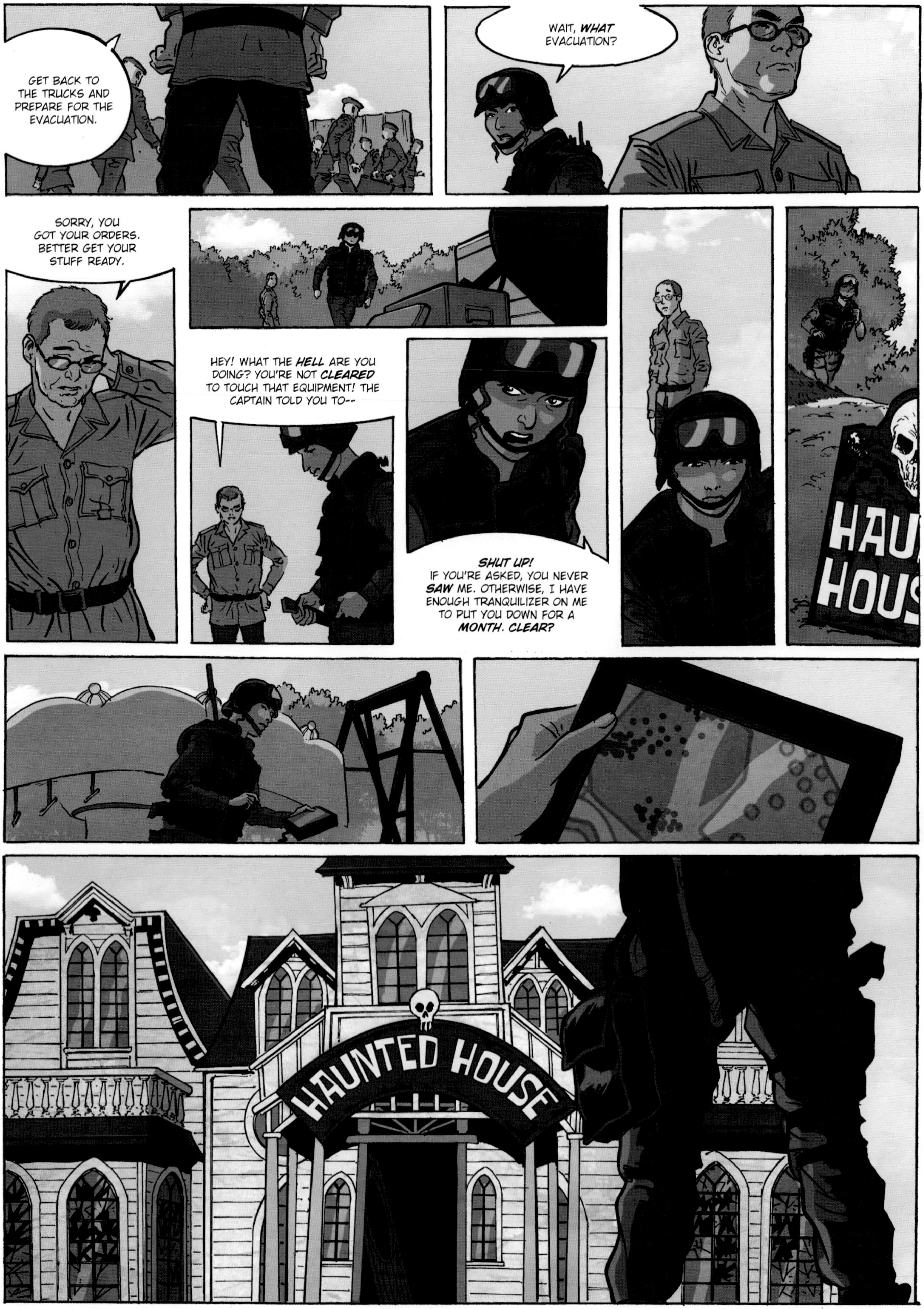
GET BACK TO THE TRUCKS AND PREPARE FOR THE EVACUATION.
WAIT, WHAT EVACUATION?
SORRY, YOU GOT YOUR ORDERS. BETTER GET YOUR STUFF READY.
HEY! WHAT THE HELL ARE YOU DOING? YOU'RE NOT CLEARED TO TOUCH THAT EQUIPMENT! THE CAPTAIN TOLD YOU TO--
SHUT UP! IF YOU'RE ASKED, YOU NEVER SAW ME. OTHERWISE, I HAVE ENOUGH TRANQUILIZER ON ME TO PUT YOU DOWN FOR A MONTH. CLEAR?
HAUNTED HOUSE

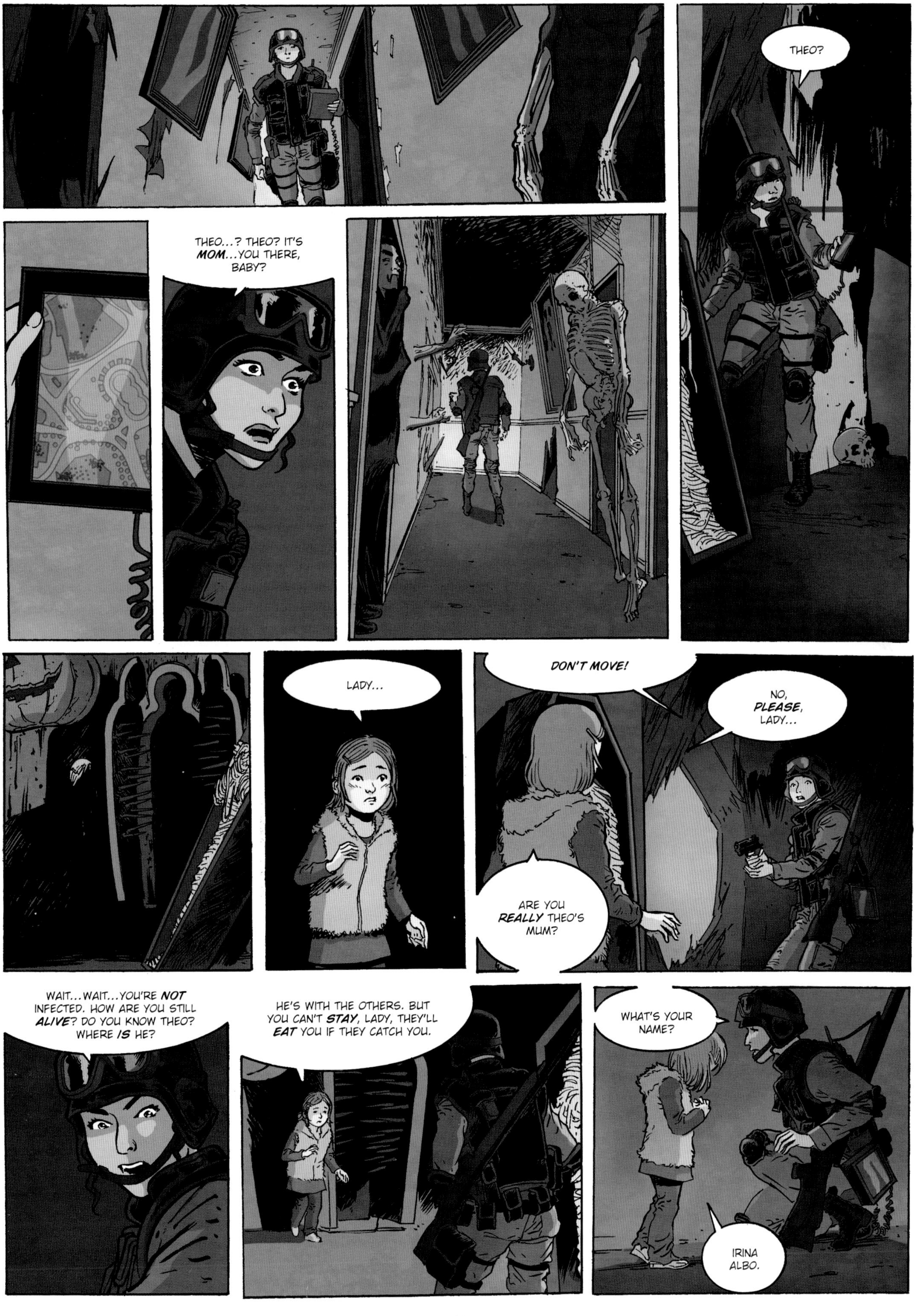
THEO?
THEO...? THEO? IT'S MOM...YOU THERE, BABY?
LADY...
DON'T MOVE!
NO, PLEASE, LADY...
ARE YOU REALLY THEO'S MUM?
WAIT...WAIT...YOU'RE NOT INFECTED. HOW ARE YOU STILL ALIVE? DO YOU KNOW THEO? WHERE IS HE?
HE'S WITH THE OTHERS. BUT YOU CAN'T STAY, LADY, THEY'LL EAT YOU IF THEY CATCH YOU.
WHAT'S YOUR NAME?
IRINA ALBO.

WHAT ARE YOU *DOING* HERE, IRINA? HOW ARE YOU NOT *SICK* LIKE THE OTHER CHILDREN?

POOR DARLING...

...LISTEN. I'M HERE TO FIND THEO AND BRING HIM HOME. WHY DON'T YOU COME WITH ME?

WHEN THEY TOOK THE SICK ONES AWAY, THEY TOOK ME TOO... MY PARENTS WEREN'T THERE BECAUSE MY BROTHER HAD *EATEN* THEM.

AND THEN YOU CAN HELP ME HELP THE DOCTORS CURE ALL THE CHILDREN?

FIRST, THOUGH, YOU HAVE TO TAKE ME TO THEO. OKAY?

OKAY. COME WITH ME.

THIS WAY.

WHEN THE SOLDIERS CAME, THEY ALL HID UNDER THE ROLLERCOASTER. THEY WERE SCARED, THEY DON'T LIKE THE NOISE -- IT HURTS THEM. THEO IS WITH THEM.

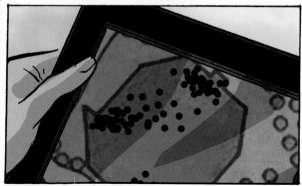

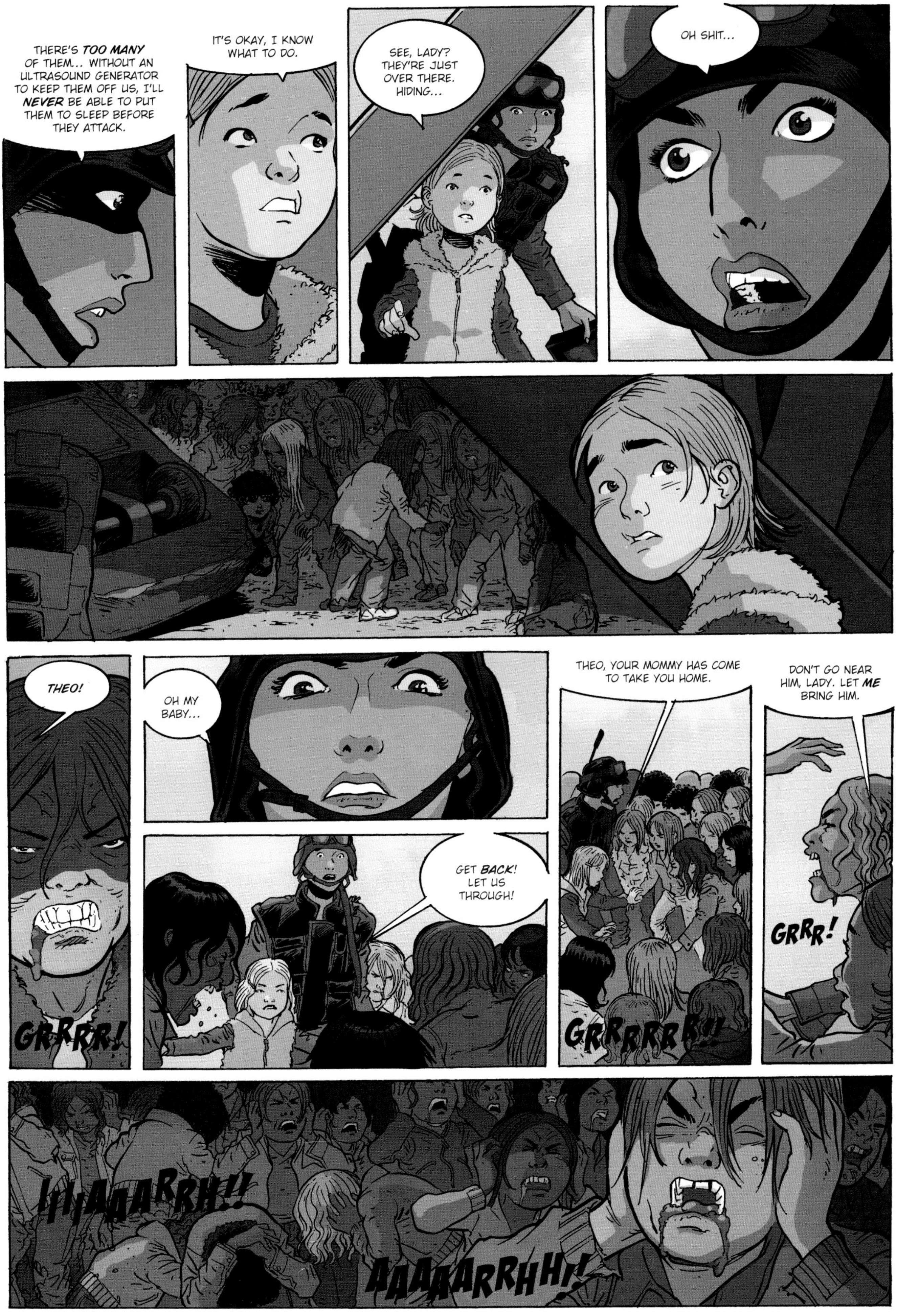
THERE'S TOO MANY OF THEM... WITHOUT AN ULTRASOUND GENERATOR TO KEEP THEM OFF US, I'LL NEVER BE ABLE TO PUT THEM TO SLEEP BEFORE THEY ATTACK.
IT'S OKAY, I KNOW WHAT TO DO.
SEE, LADY? THEY'RE JUST OVER THERE. HIDING...
OH SHIT...
THEO!
GRRRR!
OH MY BABY...
GET BACK! LET US THROUGH!
THEO, YOUR MOMMY HAS COME TO TAKE YOU HOME.
GRRRRRR!!
DON'T GO NEAR HIM, LADY. LET ME BRING HIM.
GRRR!
IIIAAAARRH!!
AAAAARRHH!!

THEO!

IT'S THE ULTRASOUNDS!

IIIAAAAAARRH!

OKAY, WE GOT CHUCKIES UNDER THE ROLLERCOASTER! CHECK AMONGST THE SCAFFOLDING, PULL THEM UP ON SCREEN, ISOLATE THEM AND KNOCK 'EM *DOWN*!

QUICK -- THIS WAY! THEY'RE COMING!

WE CAN HIDE IN THE ROLLER-COASTER.

STAY CLOSE TO ME. I HAVE TO GET YOU BACK TO THE HELICOPTER.

SHIT, THEY'RE BACK ALREADY... AND... WHY ARE THEY PUTTING THE REMOVALS IN TRUCKS? THEY *NEVER* GO IN TRUCKS.

OKAY, IRINA. I'LL GO AHEAD WITH THEO. WHEN I SIGNAL, GET ON THE HELICOPTER. YOU *CAN'T* BE SEEN, OKAY?

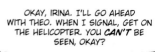

INSIDE, YOU'LL SEE A BIG BOX WITH A RED CROSS ON IT.

GET INSIDE, SHUT THE LID AND STAY *QUIET*, UNDERSTOOD?

YES, LADY.

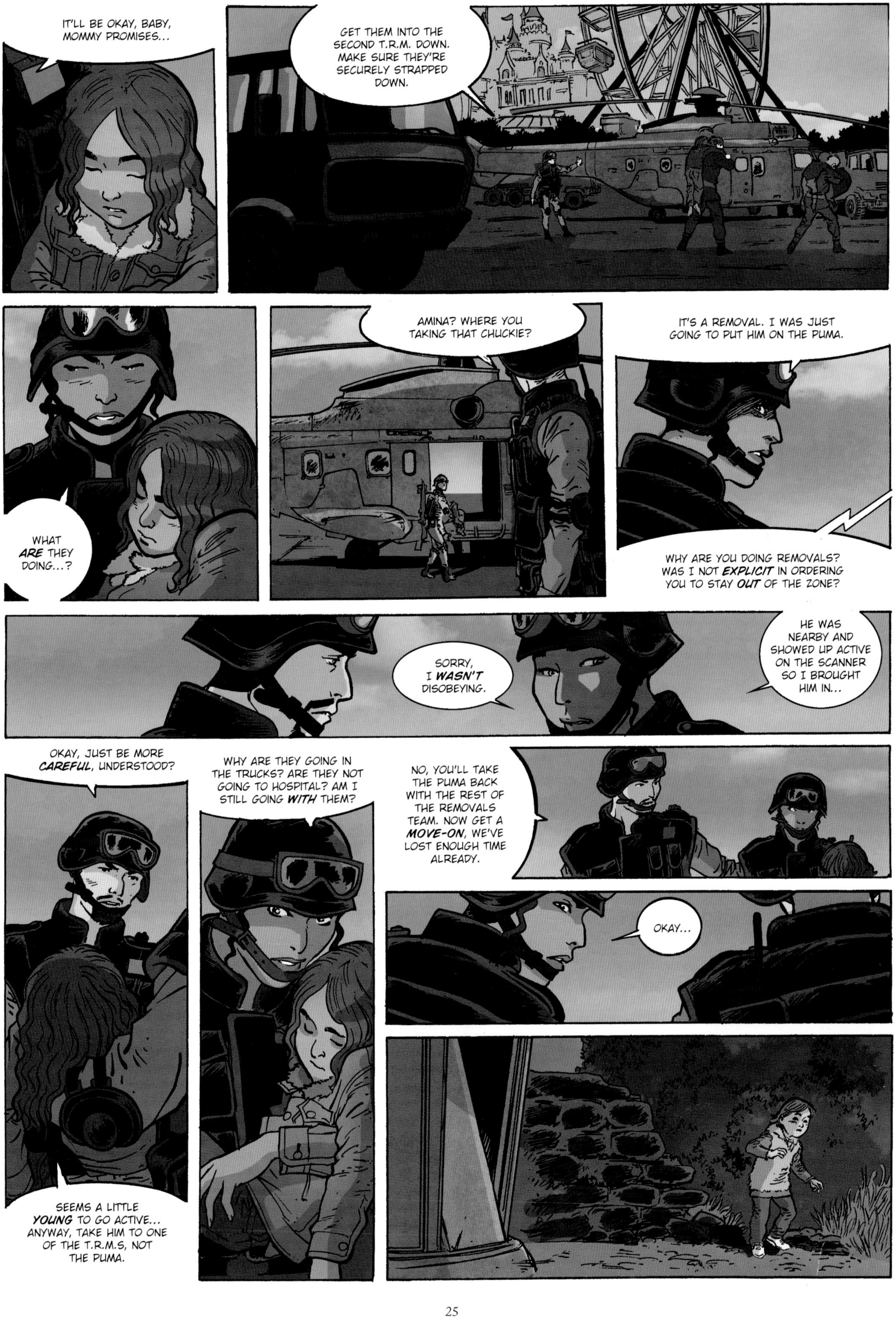
IT'LL BE OKAY, BABY, MOMMY PROMISES...
GET THEM INTO THE SECOND T.R.M. DOWN. MAKE SURE THEY'RE SECURELY STRAPPED DOWN.
WHAT ARE THEY DOING...?
AMINA? WHERE YOU TAKING THAT CHUCKIE?
IT'S A REMOVAL. I WAS JUST GOING TO PUT HIM ON THE PUMA.
WHY ARE YOU DOING REMOVALS? WAS I NOT EXPLICIT IN ORDERING YOU TO STAY OUT OF THE ZONE?
SORRY, I WASN'T DISOBEYING.
HE WAS NEARBY AND SHOWED UP ACTIVE ON THE SCANNER SO I BROUGHT HIM IN...
OKAY, JUST BE MORE CAREFUL, UNDERSTOOD?
SEEMS A LITTLE YOUNG TO GO ACTIVE... ANYWAY, TAKE HIM TO ONE OF THE T.R.M.S, NOT THE PUMA.
WHY ARE THEY GOING IN THE TRUCKS? ARE THEY NOT GOING TO HOSPITAL? AM I STILL GOING WITH THEM?
NO, YOU'LL TAKE THE PUMA BACK WITH THE REST OF THE REMOVALS TEAM. NOW GET A MOVE-ON, WE'VE LOST ENOUGH TIME ALREADY.
OKAY...

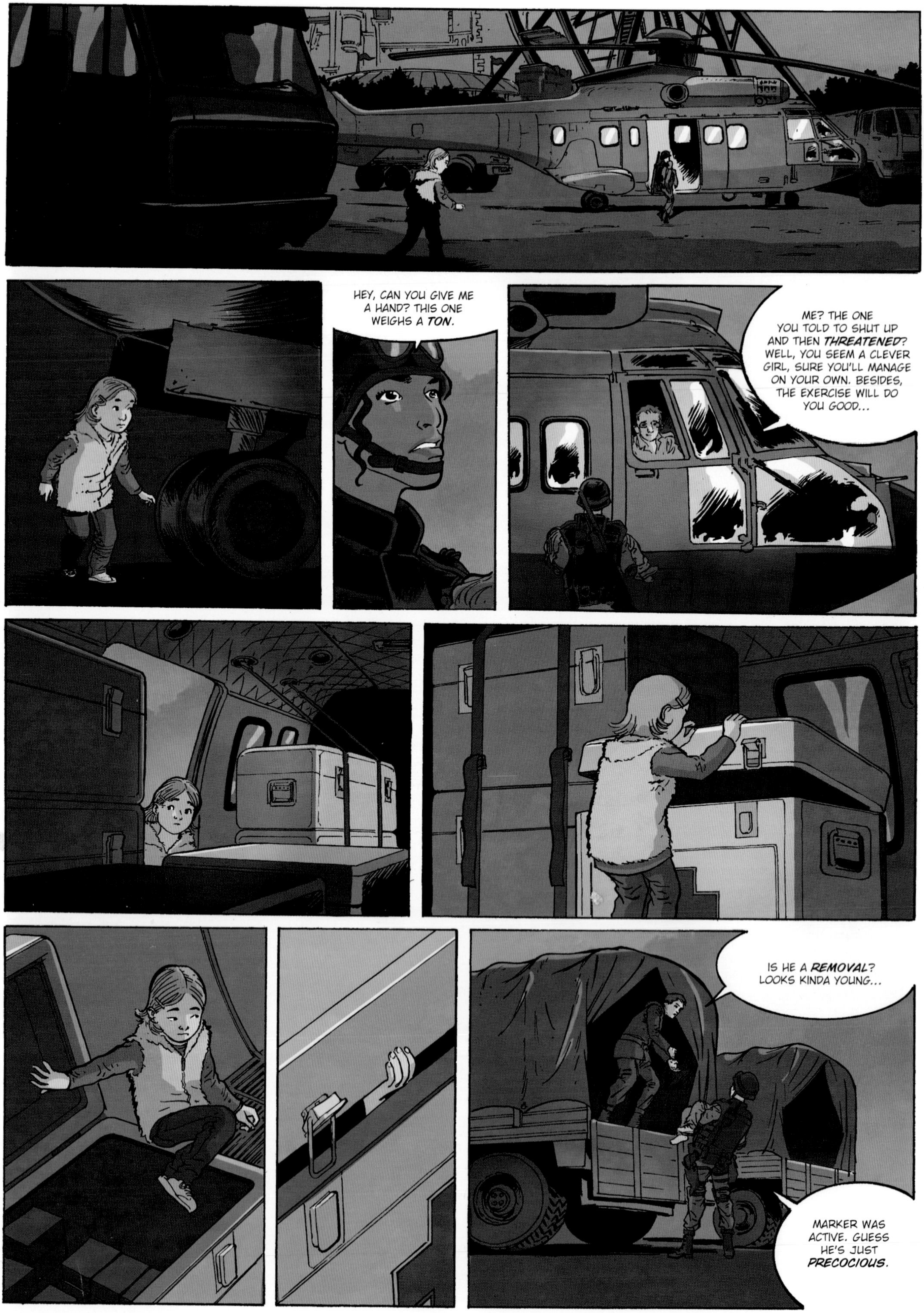
HEY, CAN YOU GIVE ME A HAND? THIS ONE WEIGHS A **TON**.
ME? THE ONE YOU TOLD TO SHUT UP AND THEN **THREATENED**? WELL, YOU SEEM A CLEVER GIRL, SURE YOU'LL MANAGE ON YOUR OWN. BESIDES, THE EXERCISE WILL DO YOU GOOD...
IS HE A **REMOVAL**? LOOKS KINDA YOUNG...
MARKER WAS ACTIVE. GUESS HE'S JUST **PRECOCIOUS**.

YOU'RE NOT REMOVING THEM WITHOUT MEDICAL SUPERVISION, ARE YOU?

WHO THE HELL IS SHE? SEEMS RATHER *NOSEY*.

SHE'S MY TEAM'S NURSE. SHOULD HAVE LEFT HER BACK IN THE GREEN ZONE...

HERE, LET ME GIVE YOU A HAND.

TAKE THIS ONE AND HE PUT HIM IN THE TRUCK WITH THE REST. WE'LL SORT HIM OUT LATER.

AND *YOU*! GET BACK TO THE PUMA AND STAY THERE. AND THIS TIME, JUST TO *CLARIFY*, IT'S AN *ORDER*!

LISTEN *UP*! WE'RE DONE HERE. REMOVALS TEAM WILL DUST OFF IN THE CHOPPER, I'LL FOLLOW ON WITH MILLER AND THE KIDS. DEBRIEF AT OH EIGHT HUNDRED. *LET'S ROLL*!

THE CAPTAIN ISN'T COMING BACK WITH US?

APPARENTLY NOT. I'M STILL NOT ACTUALLY SURE WHY HE MADE US *COME* IN THE FIRST PLACE...

HEY, AMINA. YOU *OKAY*? YOU LOOK A LITTLE PALE...

I'M FINE... JUST A LITTLE WORN OUT...

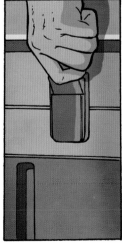

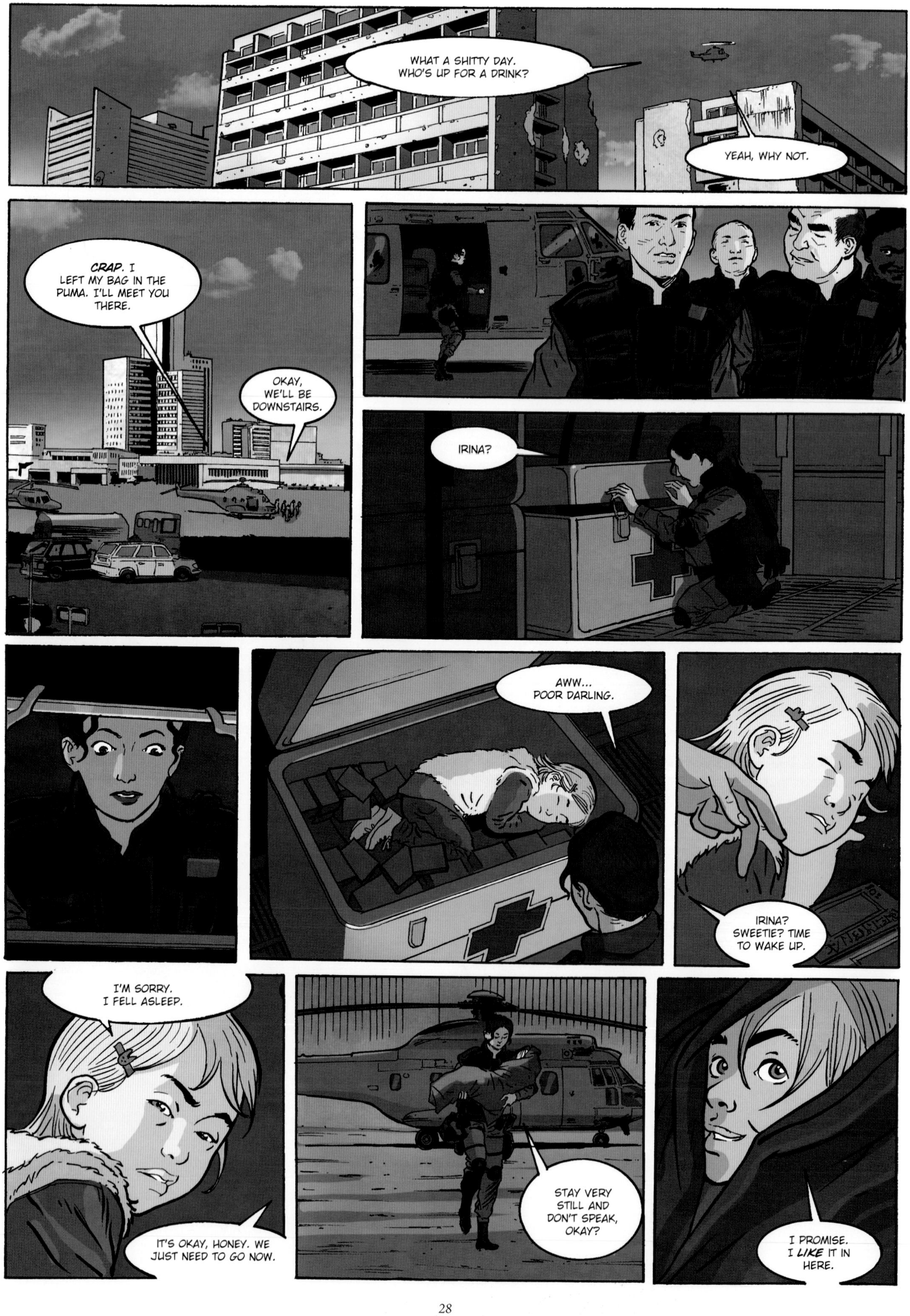
WHAT A SHITTY DAY. WHO'S UP FOR A DRINK?
YEAH, WHY NOT.
CRAP. I LEFT MY BAG IN THE PUMA. I'LL MEET YOU THERE.
OKAY, WE'LL BE DOWNSTAIRS.
IRINA?
AWW... POOR DARLING.
IRINA? SWEETIE? TIME TO WAKE UP.
I'M SORRY. I FELL ASLEEP.
IT'S OKAY, HONEY. WE JUST NEED TO GO NOW.
STAY VERY STILL AND DON'T SPEAK, OKAY?
I PROMISE. I LIKE IT IN HERE.

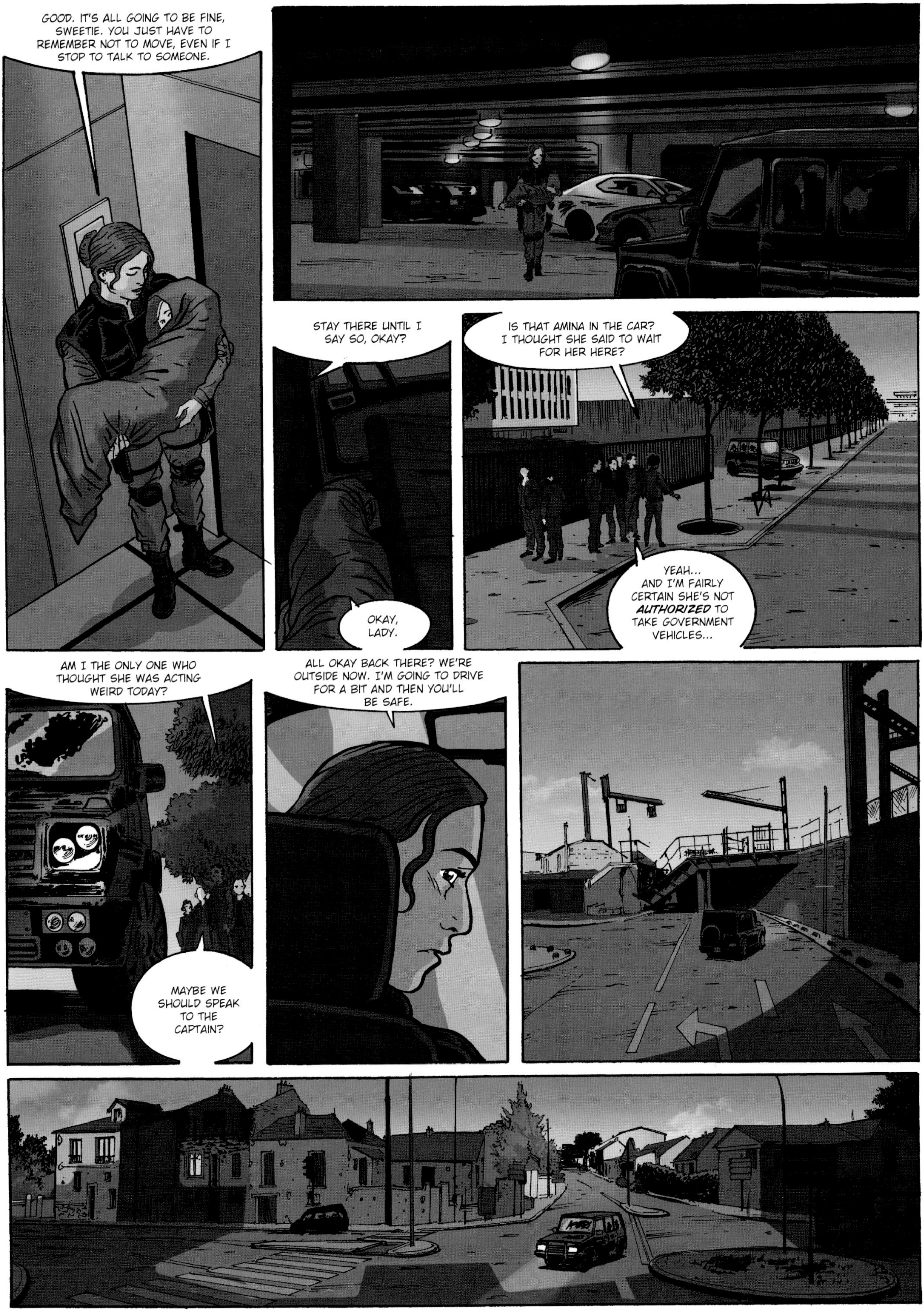
GOOD. IT'S ALL GOING TO BE FINE, SWEETIE. YOU JUST HAVE TO REMEMBER NOT TO MOVE, EVEN IF I STOP TO TALK TO SOMEONE.
STAY THERE UNTIL I SAY SO, OKAY?
OKAY, LADY.
IS THAT AMINA IN THE CAR? I THOUGHT SHE SAID TO WAIT FOR HER HERE?
YEAH... AND I'M FAIRLY CERTAIN SHE'S NOT AUTHORIZED TO TAKE GOVERNMENT VEHICLES...
AM I THE ONLY ONE WHO THOUGHT SHE WAS ACTING WEIRD TODAY?
MAYBE WE SHOULD SPEAK TO THE CAPTAIN?
ALL OKAY BACK THERE? WE'RE OUTSIDE NOW. I'M GOING TO DRIVE FOR A BIT AND THEN YOU'LL BE SAFE.

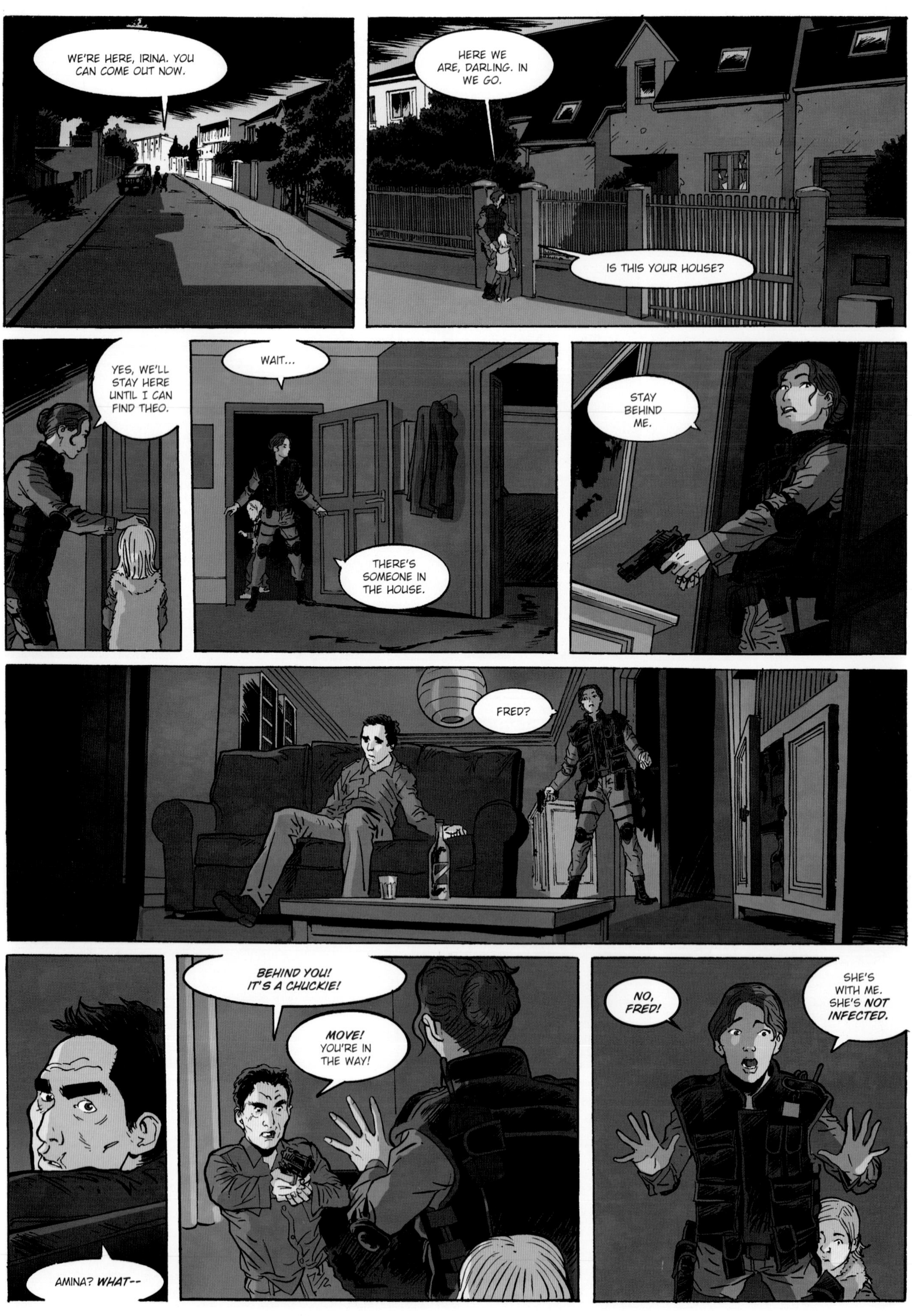
WE'RE HERE, IRINA. YOU CAN COME OUT NOW.
HERE WE ARE, DARLING. IN WE GO.
IS THIS YOUR HOUSE?
YES, WE'LL STAY HERE UNTIL I CAN FIND THEO.
WAIT...
THERE'S SOMEONE IN THE HOUSE.
STAY BEHIND ME.
FRED?
AMINA? WHAT--
BEHIND YOU! IT'S A CHUCKIE!
MOVE! YOU'RE IN THE WAY!
NO, FRED!
SHE'S WITH ME. SHE'S NOT INFECTED.

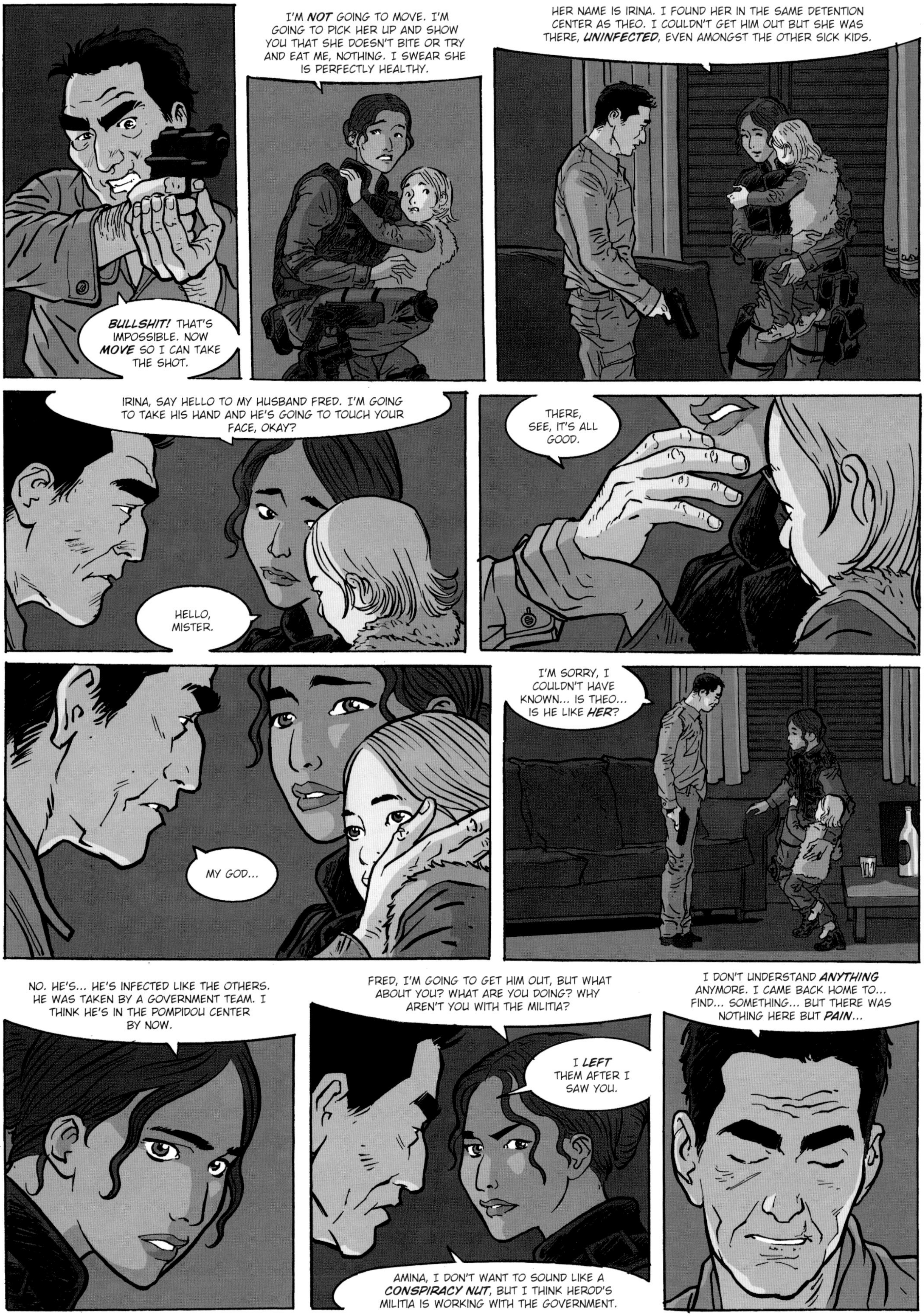
BULLSHIT! THAT'S IMPOSSIBLE. NOW MOVE SO I CAN TAKE THE SHOT.
I'M NOT GOING TO MOVE. I'M GOING TO PICK HER UP AND SHOW YOU THAT SHE DOESN'T BITE OR TRY AND EAT ME, NOTHING. I SWEAR SHE IS PERFECTLY HEALTHY.
HER NAME IS IRINA. I FOUND HER IN THE SAME DETENTION CENTER AS THEO. I COULDN'T GET HIM OUT BUT SHE WAS THERE, UNINFECTED, EVEN AMONGST THE OTHER SICK KIDS.
IRINA, SAY HELLO TO MY HUSBAND FRED. I'M GOING TO TAKE HIS HAND AND HE'S GOING TO TOUCH YOUR FACE, OKAY?
HELLO, MISTER.
THERE, SEE, IT'S ALL GOOD.
MY GOD...
I'M SORRY, I COULDN'T HAVE KNOWN... IS THEO... IS HE LIKE HER?
NO. HE'S... HE'S INFECTED LIKE THE OTHERS. HE WAS TAKEN BY A GOVERNMENT TEAM. I THINK HE'S IN THE POMPIDOU CENTER BY NOW.
FRED, I'M GOING TO GET HIM OUT, BUT WHAT ABOUT YOU? WHAT ARE YOU DOING? WHY AREN'T YOU WITH THE MILITIA?
I LEFT THEM AFTER I SAW YOU.
AMINA, I DON'T WANT TO SOUND LIKE A CONSPIRACY NUT, BUT I THINK HEROD'S MILITIA IS WORKING WITH THE GOVERNMENT.
I DON'T UNDERSTAND ANYTHING ANYMORE. I CAME BACK HOME TO... FIND... SOMETHING... BUT THERE WAS NOTHING HERE BUT PAIN...

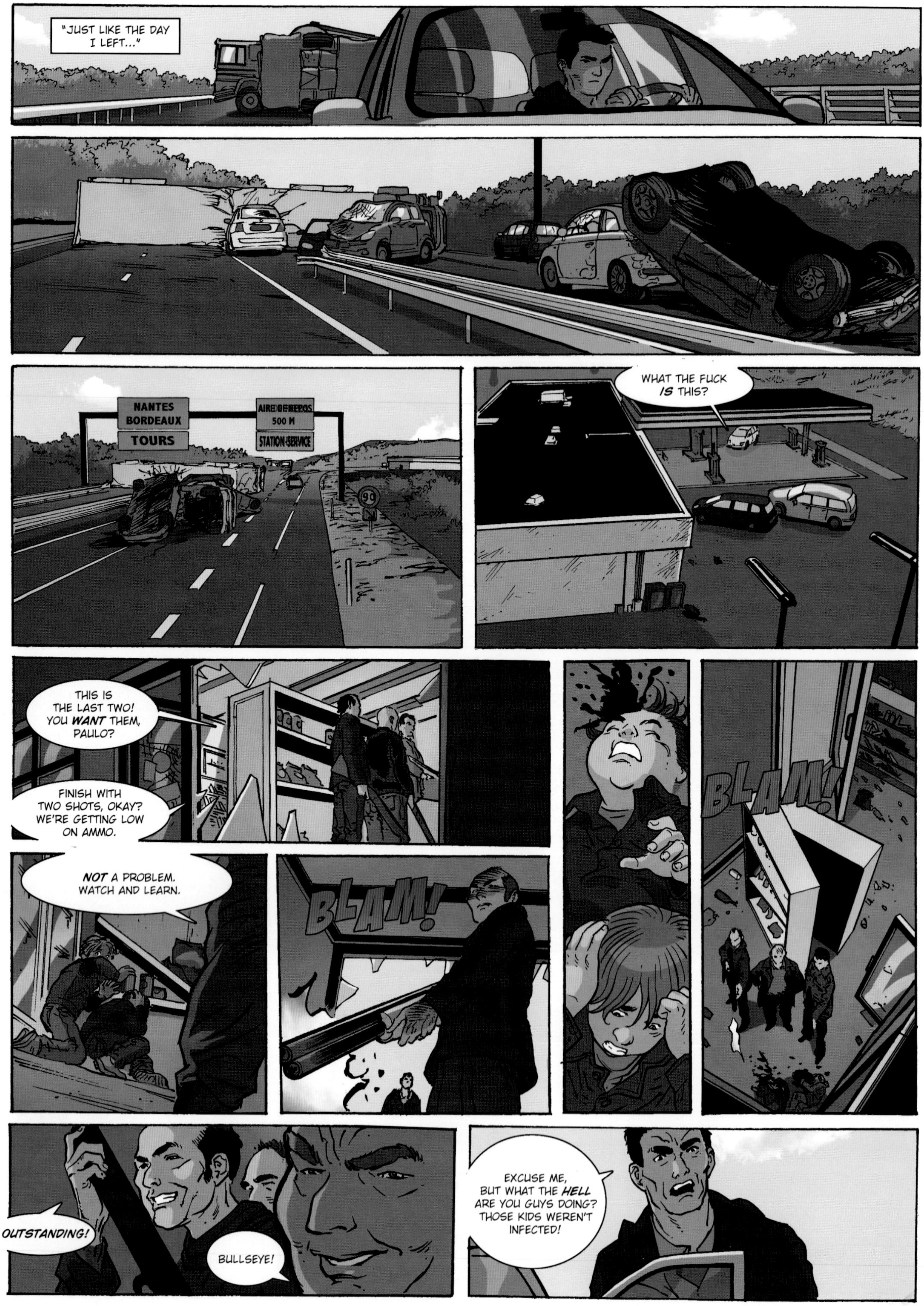
"JUST LIKE THE DAY I LEFT..."
NANTES BORDEAUX
TOURS
AIRE DE REPOS 500 M
STATION SERVICE
90
WHAT THE FUCK *IS* THIS?
THIS IS THE LAST TWO! YOU *WANT* THEM, PAULO?
FINISH WITH TWO SHOTS, OKAY? WE'RE GETTING LOW ON AMMO.
NOT A PROBLEM. WATCH AND LEARN.
BLAM!
BLAM!
OUTSTANDING!
BULLSEYE!
EXCUSE ME, BUT WHAT THE *HELL* ARE YOU GUYS DOING? THOSE KIDS WEREN'T INFECTED!

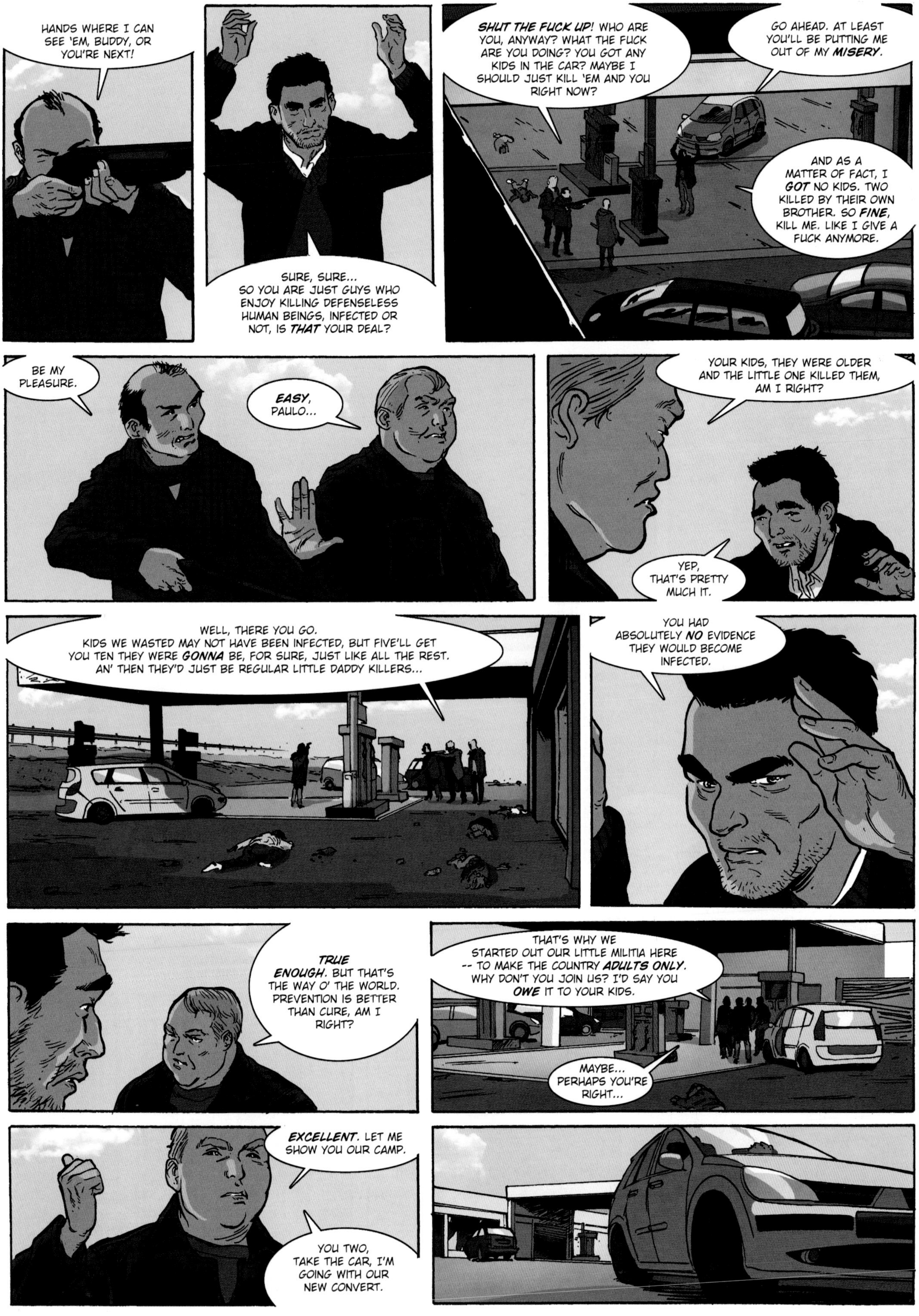
HANDS WHERE I CAN SEE 'EM, BUDDY, OR YOU'RE NEXT!
SURE, SURE... SO YOU ARE JUST GUYS WHO ENJOY KILLING DEFENSELESS HUMAN BEINGS, INFECTED OR NOT, IS THAT YOUR DEAL?
SHUT THE FUCK UP! WHO ARE YOU, ANYWAY? WHAT THE FUCK ARE YOU DOING? YOU GOT ANY KIDS IN THE CAR? MAYBE I SHOULD JUST KILL 'EM AND YOU RIGHT NOW?
GO AHEAD. AT LEAST YOU'LL BE PUTTING ME OUT OF MY MISERY.
AND AS A MATTER OF FACT, I GOT NO KIDS. TWO KILLED BY THEIR OWN BROTHER. SO FINE, KILL ME. LIKE I GIVE A FUCK ANYMORE.
BE MY PLEASURE.
EASY, PAULO...
YOUR KIDS, THEY WERE OLDER AND THE LITTLE ONE KILLED THEM, AM I RIGHT?
YEP, THAT'S PRETTY MUCH IT.
WELL, THERE YOU GO. KIDS WE WASTED MAY NOT HAVE BEEN INFECTED, BUT FIVE'LL GET YOU TEN THEY WERE GONNA BE, FOR SURE, JUST LIKE ALL THE REST. AN' THEN THEY'D JUST BE REGULAR LITTLE DADDY KILLERS...
YOU HAD ABSOLUTELY NO EVIDENCE THEY WOULD BECOME INFECTED.
TRUE ENOUGH. BUT THAT'S THE WAY O' THE WORLD. PREVENTION IS BETTER THAN CURE, AM I RIGHT?
THAT'S WHY WE STARTED OUT OUR LITTLE MILITIA HERE -- TO MAKE THE COUNTRY ADULTS ONLY. WHY DON'T YOU JOIN US? I'D SAY YOU OWE IT TO YOUR KIDS.
MAYBE... PERHAPS YOU'RE RIGHT...
EXCELLENT. LET ME SHOW YOU OUR CAMP.
YOU TWO, TAKE THE CAR, I'M GOING WITH OUR NEW CONVERT.

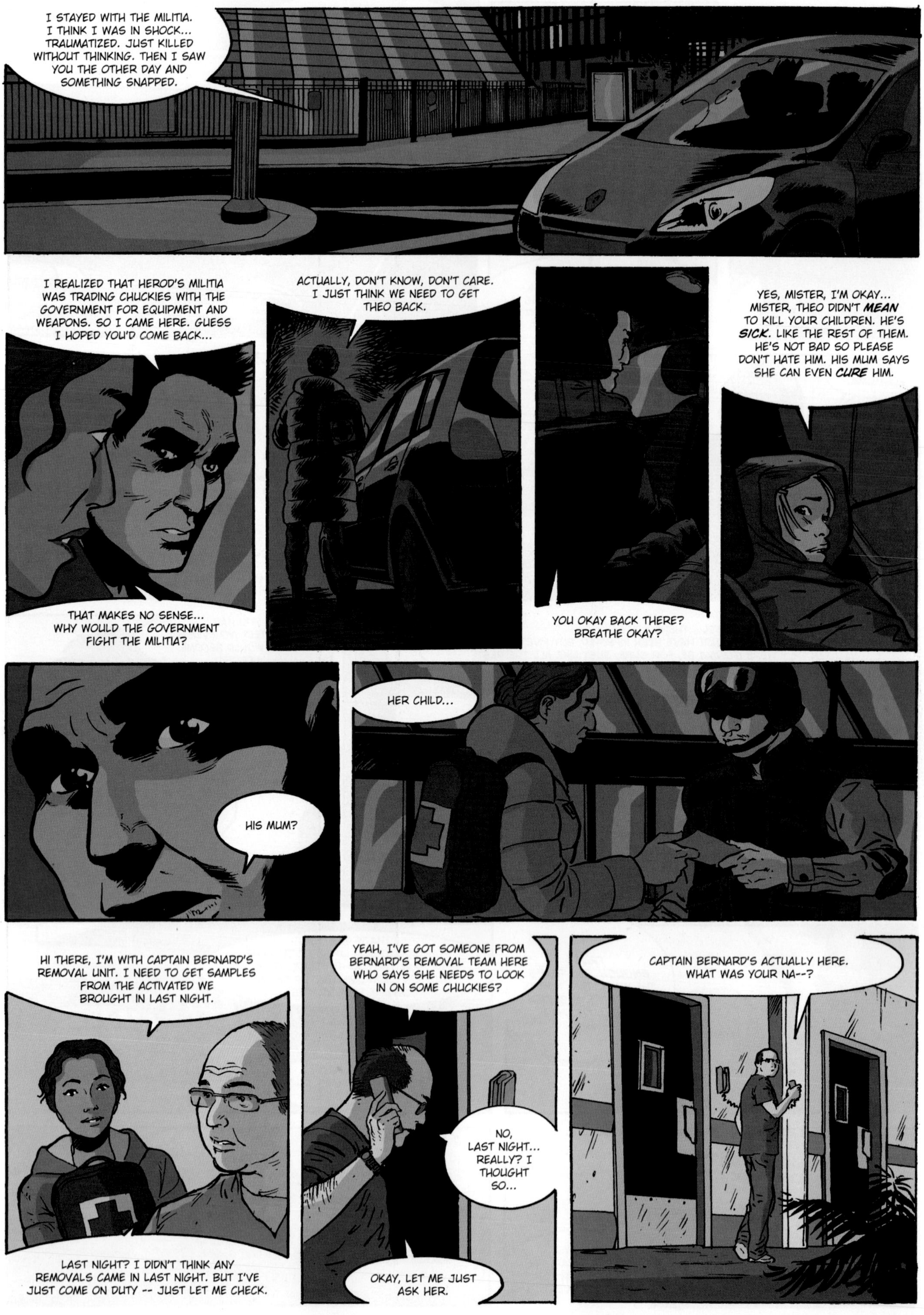
I STAYED WITH THE MILITIA. I THINK I WAS IN SHOCK... TRAUMATIZED. JUST KILLED WITHOUT THINKING. THEN I SAW YOU THE OTHER DAY AND SOMETHING SNAPPED.
I REALIZED THAT HEROD'S MILITIA WAS TRADING CHUCKIES WITH THE GOVERNMENT FOR EQUIPMENT AND WEAPONS. SO I CAME HERE. GUESS I HOPED YOU'D COME BACK...
THAT MAKES NO SENSE... WHY WOULD THE GOVERNMENT FIGHT THE MILITIA?
ACTUALLY, DON'T KNOW, DON'T CARE. I JUST THINK WE NEED TO GET THEO BACK.
YOU OKAY BACK THERE? BREATHE OKAY?
YES, MISTER, I'M OKAY... MISTER, THEO DIDN'T MEAN TO KILL YOUR CHILDREN. HE'S SICK. LIKE THE REST OF THEM. HE'S NOT BAD SO PLEASE DON'T HATE HIM. HIS MUM SAYS SHE CAN EVEN CURE HIM.
HIS MUM?
HER CHILD...
HI THERE, I'M WITH CAPTAIN BERNARD'S REMOVAL UNIT. I NEED TO GET SAMPLES FROM THE ACTIVATED WE BROUGHT IN LAST NIGHT.
LAST NIGHT? I DIDN'T THINK ANY REMOVALS CAME IN LAST NIGHT. BUT I'VE JUST COME ON DUTY -- JUST LET ME CHECK.
YEAH, I'VE GOT SOMEONE FROM BERNARD'S REMOVAL TEAM HERE WHO SAYS SHE NEEDS TO LOOK IN ON SOME CHUCKIES?
NO, LAST NIGHT... REALLY? I THOUGHT SO...
OKAY, LET ME JUST ASK HER.
CAPTAIN BERNARD'S ACTUALLY HERE. WHAT WAS YOUR NA--?

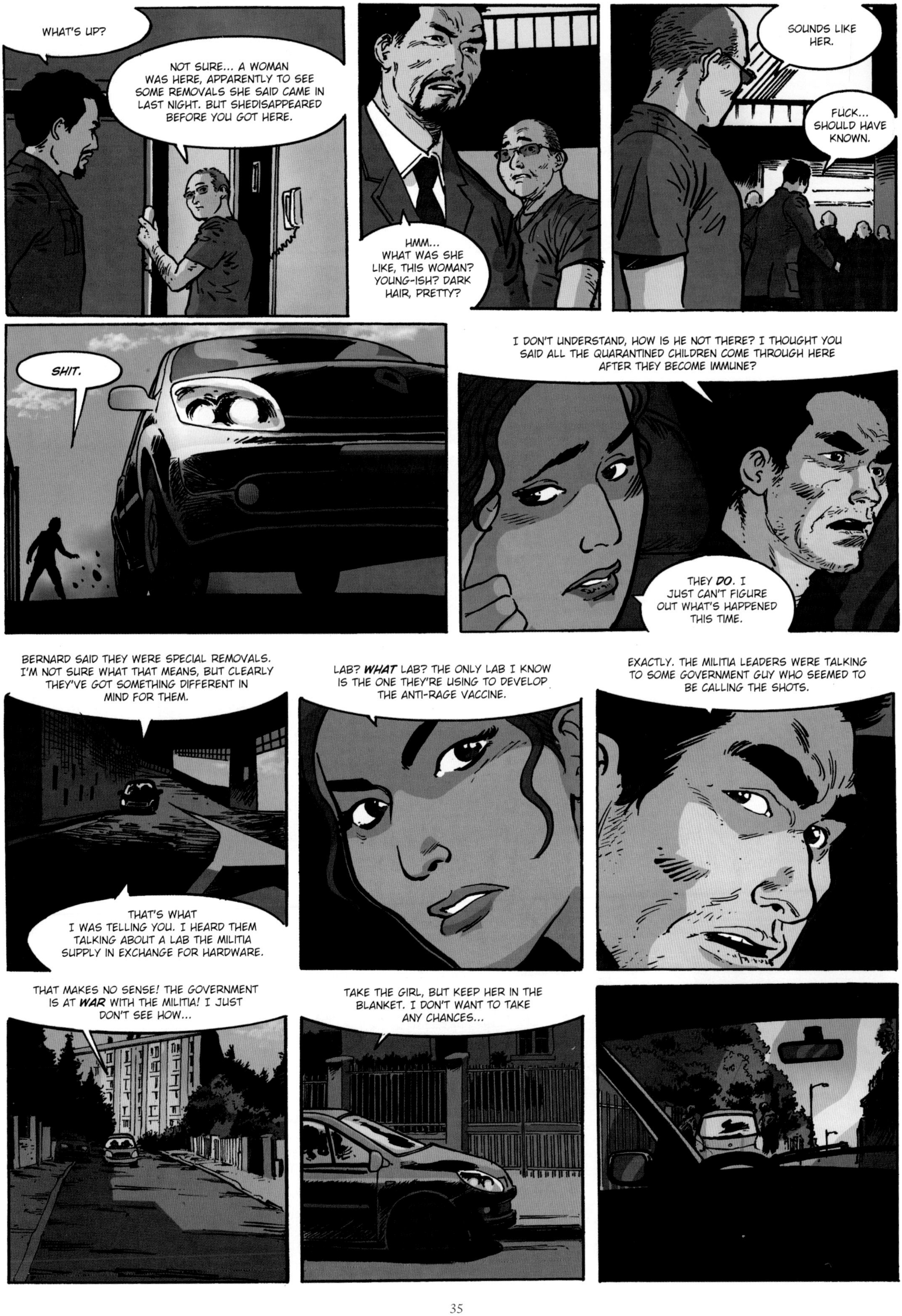
WHAT'S UP?
NOT SURE... A WOMAN WAS HERE, APPARENTLY TO SEE SOME REMOVALS SHE SAID CAME IN LAST NIGHT. BUT SHEDISAPPEARED BEFORE YOU GOT HERE.
HMM... WHAT WAS SHE LIKE, THIS WOMAN? YOUNG-ISH? DARK HAIR, PRETTY?
SOUNDS LIKE HER.
FUCK... SHOULD HAVE KNOWN.
SHIT.
I DON'T UNDERSTAND, HOW IS HE NOT THERE? I THOUGHT YOU SAID ALL THE QUARANTINED CHILDREN COME THROUGH HERE AFTER THEY BECOME IMMUNE?
THEY DO. I JUST CAN'T FIGURE OUT WHAT'S HAPPENED THIS TIME.
BERNARD SAID THEY WERE SPECIAL REMOVALS. I'M NOT SURE WHAT THAT MEANS, BUT CLEARLY THEY'VE GOT SOMETHING DIFFERENT IN MIND FOR THEM.
THAT'S WHAT I WAS TELLING YOU. I HEARD THEM TALKING ABOUT A LAB THE MILITIA SUPPLY IN EXCHANGE FOR HARDWARE.
LAB? WHAT LAB? THE ONLY LAB I KNOW IS THE ONE THEY'RE USING TO DEVELOP THE ANTI-RAGE VACCINE.
EXACTLY. THE MILITIA LEADERS WERE TALKING TO SOME GOVERNMENT GUY WHO SEEMED TO BE CALLING THE SHOTS.
THAT MAKES NO SENSE! THE GOVERNMENT IS AT WAR WITH THE MILITIA! I JUST DON'T SEE HOW...
TAKE THE GIRL, BUT KEEP HER IN THE BLANKET. I DON'T WANT TO TAKE ANY CHANCES...

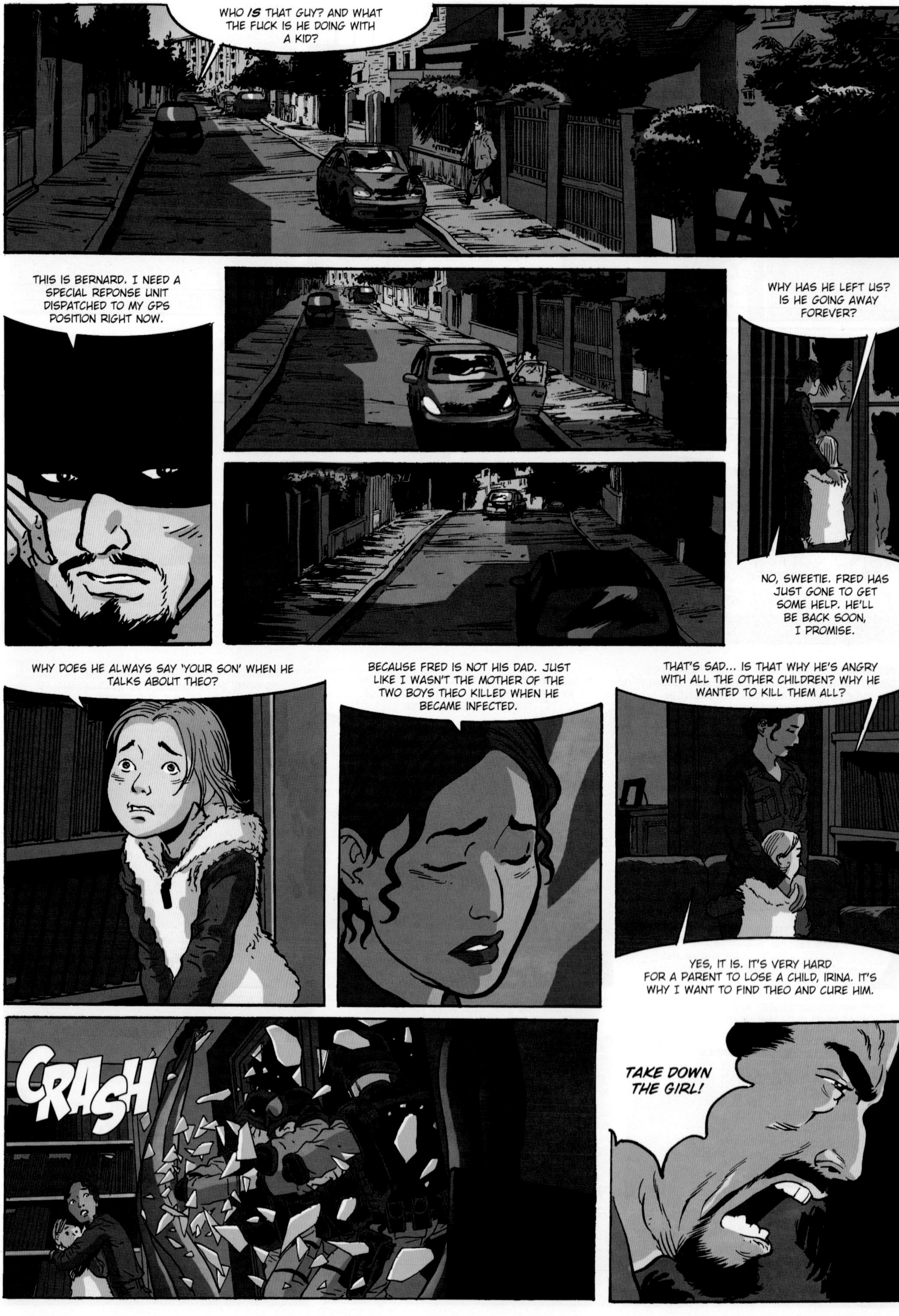
WHO *IS* THAT GUY? AND WHAT THE FUCK IS HE DOING WITH A KID?
THIS IS BERNARD. I NEED A SPECIAL REPONSE UNIT DISPATCHED TO MY GPS POSITION RIGHT NOW.
WHY HAS HE LEFT US? IS HE GOING AWAY FOREVER?
NO, SWEETIE. FRED HAS JUST GONE TO GET SOME HELP. HE'LL BE BACK SOON, I PROMISE.
WHY DOES HE ALWAYS SAY 'YOUR SON' WHEN HE TALKS ABOUT THEO?
BECAUSE FRED IS NOT HIS DAD. JUST LIKE I WASN'T THE MOTHER OF THE TWO BOYS THEO KILLED WHEN HE BECAME INFECTED.
THAT'S SAD... IS THAT WHY HE'S ANGRY WITH ALL THE OTHER CHILDREN? WHY HE WANTED TO KILL THEM ALL?
YES, IT IS. IT'S VERY HARD FOR A PARENT TO LOSE A CHILD, IRINA. IT'S WHY I WANT TO FIND THEO AND CURE HIM.
CRASH
TAKE DOWN THE GIRL!

NOOOOOO!

YOU *BASTARD!* SHE HASN'T *DONE* ANYTHING!

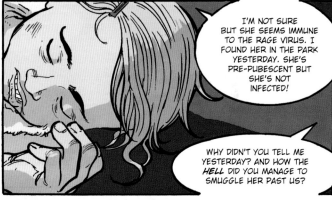

SHE'S NOT EVEN *INFECTED!*

WAIT? *WHAT?* HOW CAN SHE NOT BE INFECTED?

I'M NOT SURE BUT SHE SEEMS IMMUNE TO THE RAGE VIRUS. I FOUND HER IN THE PARK YESTERDAY. SHE'S PRE-PUBESCENT BUT SHE'S NOT INFECTED!

WHY DIDN'T YOU TELL ME YESTERDAY? AND HOW THE *HELL* DID YOU MANAGE TO SMUGGLE HER PAST US?

BECAUSE SOMETHING WASN'T *RIGHT* ABOUT THE OPERATION. I *KNOW* THOSE KIDS WEREN'T TAKEN TO THE HOSPITAL. WHERE DID YOU TAKE THEM?

ISN'T THIS MORE TO DO WITH YOU TRYING TO GET YOUR *OWN* SON BACK?

THAT'S WHO YOU WERE LOOKING FOR YESTERDAY, RIGHT? HIS MARKERS HAVEN'T GONE ACTIVE, BUT YOU STILL WANTED HIM OUT OF QUARANTINE...

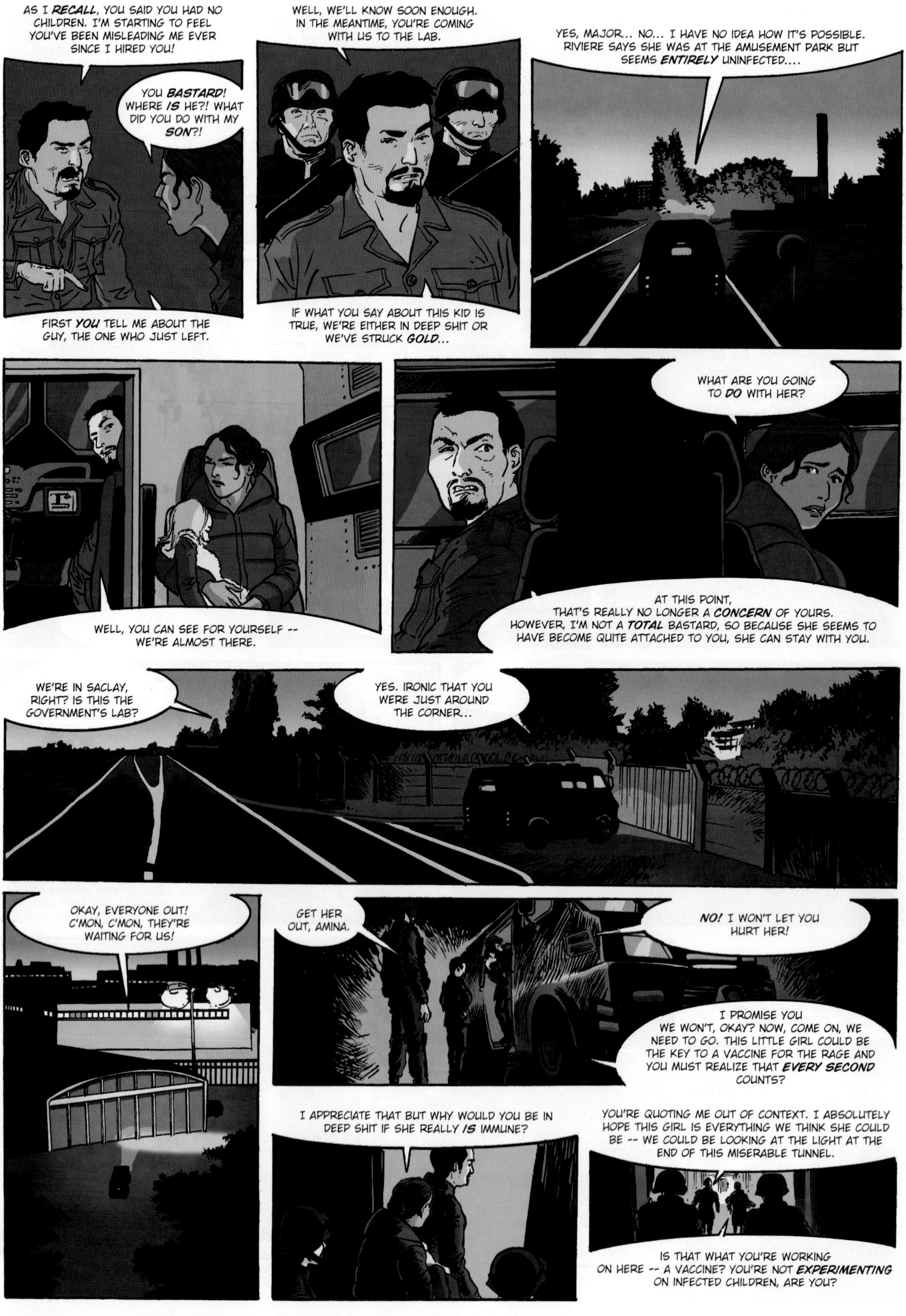
AS I RECALL, YOU SAID YOU HAD NO CHILDREN. I'M STARTING TO FEEL YOU'VE BEEN MISLEADING ME EVER SINCE I HIRED YOU!
YOU BASTARD! WHERE IS HE?! WHAT DID YOU DO WITH MY SON?!
FIRST YOU TELL ME ABOUT THE GUY, THE ONE WHO JUST LEFT.
WELL, WE'LL KNOW SOON ENOUGH. IN THE MEANTIME, YOU'RE COMING WITH US TO THE LAB.
IF WHAT YOU SAY ABOUT THIS KID IS TRUE, WE'RE EITHER IN DEEP SHIT OR WE'VE STRUCK GOLD...
YES, MAJOR... NO... I HAVE NO IDEA HOW IT'S POSSIBLE. RIVIERE SAYS SHE WAS AT THE AMUSEMENT PARK BUT SEEMS ENTIRELY UNINFECTED....
WELL, YOU CAN SEE FOR YOURSELF -- WE'RE ALMOST THERE.
WHAT ARE YOU GOING TO DO WITH HER?
AT THIS POINT, THAT'S REALLY NO LONGER A CONCERN OF YOURS. HOWEVER, I'M NOT A TOTAL BASTARD, SO BECAUSE SHE SEEMS TO HAVE BECOME QUITE ATTACHED TO YOU, SHE CAN STAY WITH YOU.
WE'RE IN SACLAY, RIGHT? IS THIS THE GOVERNMENT'S LAB?
YES. IRONIC THAT YOU WERE JUST AROUND THE CORNER...
OKAY, EVERYONE OUT! C'MON, C'MON, THEY'RE WAITING FOR US!
GET HER OUT, AMINA.
NO! I WON'T LET YOU HURT HER!
I PROMISE YOU WE WON'T, OKAY? NOW, COME ON, WE NEED TO GO. THIS LITTLE GIRL COULD BE THE KEY TO A VACCINE FOR THE RAGE AND YOU MUST REALIZE THAT EVERY SECOND COUNTS?
I APPRECIATE THAT BUT WHY WOULD YOU BE IN DEEP SHIT IF SHE REALLY IS IMMUNE?
YOU'RE QUOTING ME OUT OF CONTEXT. I ABSOLUTELY HOPE THIS GIRL IS EVERYTHING WE THINK SHE COULD BE -- WE COULD BE LOOKING AT THE LIGHT AT THE END OF THIS MISERABLE TUNNEL.
IS THAT WHAT YOU'RE WORKING ON HERE -- A VACCINE? YOU'RE NOT EXPERIMENTING ON INFECTED CHILDREN, ARE YOU?

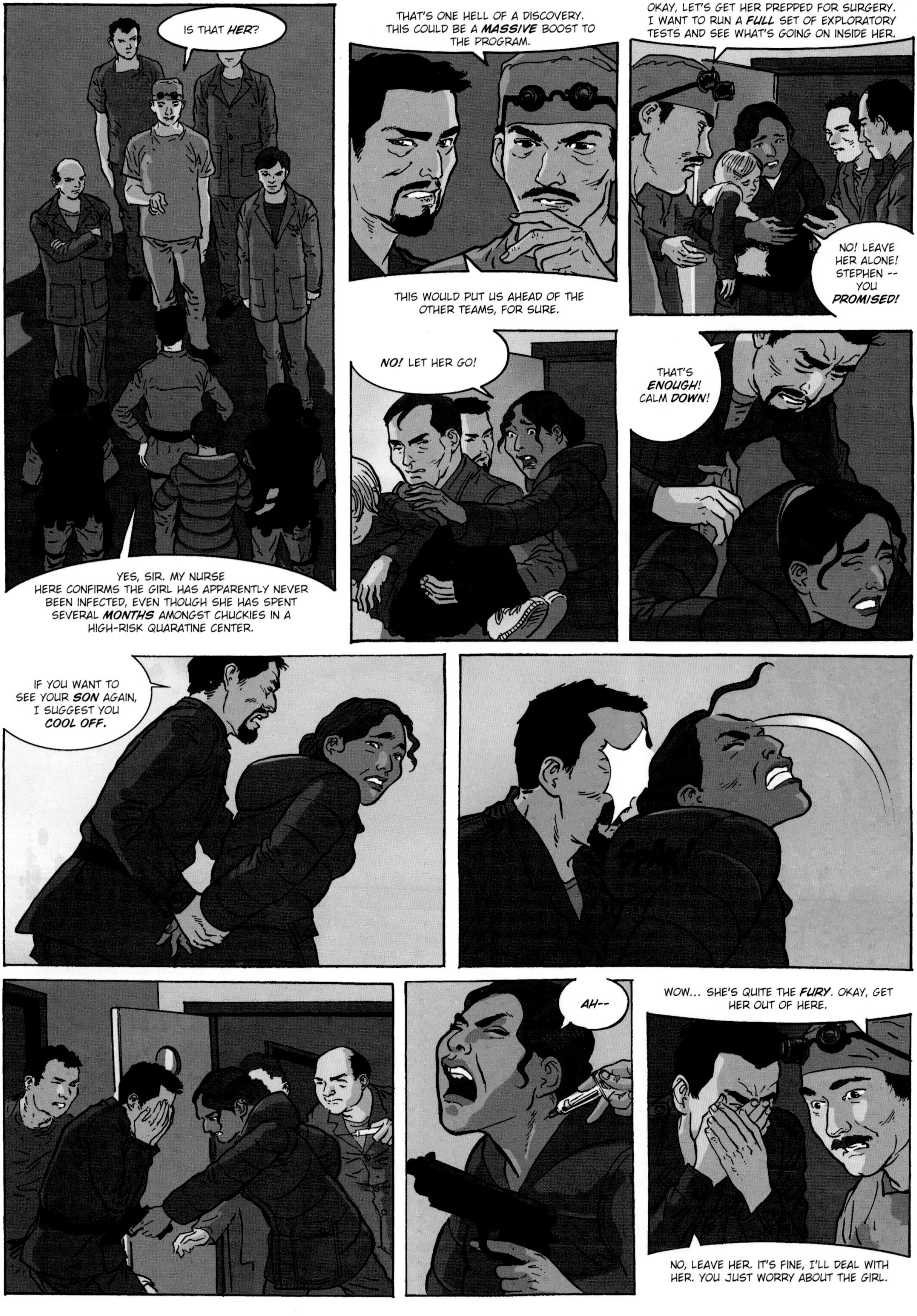
IS THAT HER?
YES, SIR. MY NURSE HERE CONFIRMS THE GIRL HAS APPARENTLY NEVER BEEN INFECTED, EVEN THOUGH SHE HAS SPENT SEVERAL MONTHS AMONGST CHUCKIES IN A HIGH-RISK QUARATINE CENTER.
THAT'S ONE HELL OF A DISCOVERY. THIS COULD BE A MASSIVE BOOST TO THE PROGRAM.
THIS WOULD PUT US AHEAD OF THE OTHER TEAMS, FOR SURE.
OKAY, LET'S GET HER PREPPED FOR SURGERY. I WANT TO RUN A FULL SET OF EXPLORATORY TESTS AND SEE WHAT'S GOING ON INSIDE HER.
NO! LEAVE HER ALONE! STEPHEN -- YOU PROMISED!
NO! LET HER GO!
THAT'S ENOUGH! CALM DOWN!
IF YOU WANT TO SEE YOUR SON AGAIN, I SUGGEST YOU COOL OFF.
SPAK!
AH--
WOW... SHE'S QUITE THE FURY. OKAY, GET HER OUT OF HERE.
NO, LEAVE HER. IT'S FINE, I'LL DEAL WITH HER. YOU JUST WORRY ABOUT THE GIRL.

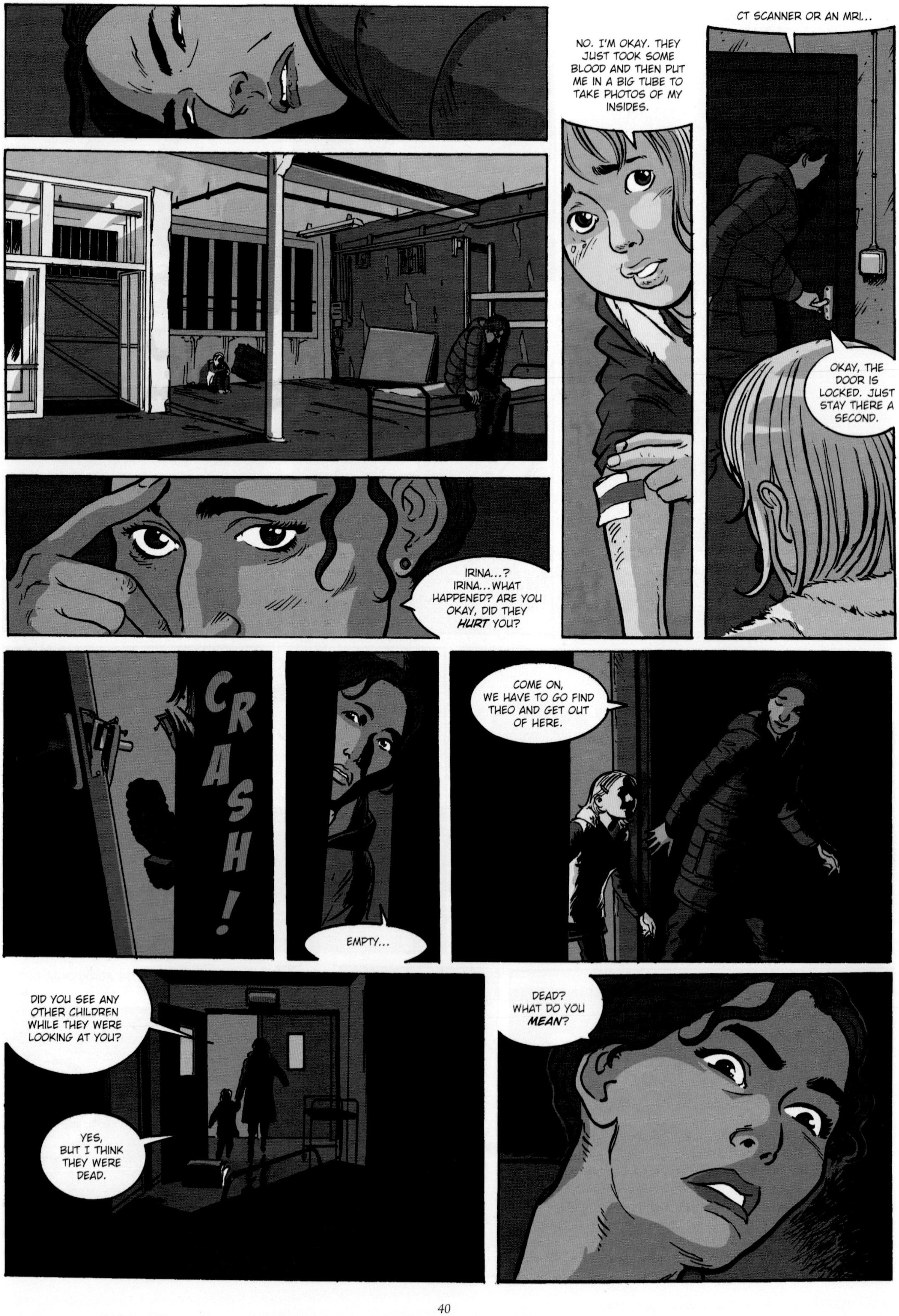
IRINA...? IRINA...WHAT HAPPENED? ARE YOU OKAY, DID THEY HURT YOU?
NO. I'M OKAY. THEY JUST TOOK SOME BLOOD AND THEN PUT ME IN A BIG TUBE TO TAKE PHOTOS OF MY INSIDES.
CT SCANNER OR AN MRI...
OKAY, THE DOOR IS LOCKED. JUST STAY THERE A SECOND.
CRASH!
EMPTY...
COME ON, WE HAVE TO GO FIND THEO AND GET OUT OF HERE.
DID YOU SEE ANY OTHER CHILDREN WHILE THEY WERE LOOKING AT YOU?
YES, BUT I THINK THEY WERE DEAD.
DEAD? WHAT DO YOU MEAN?

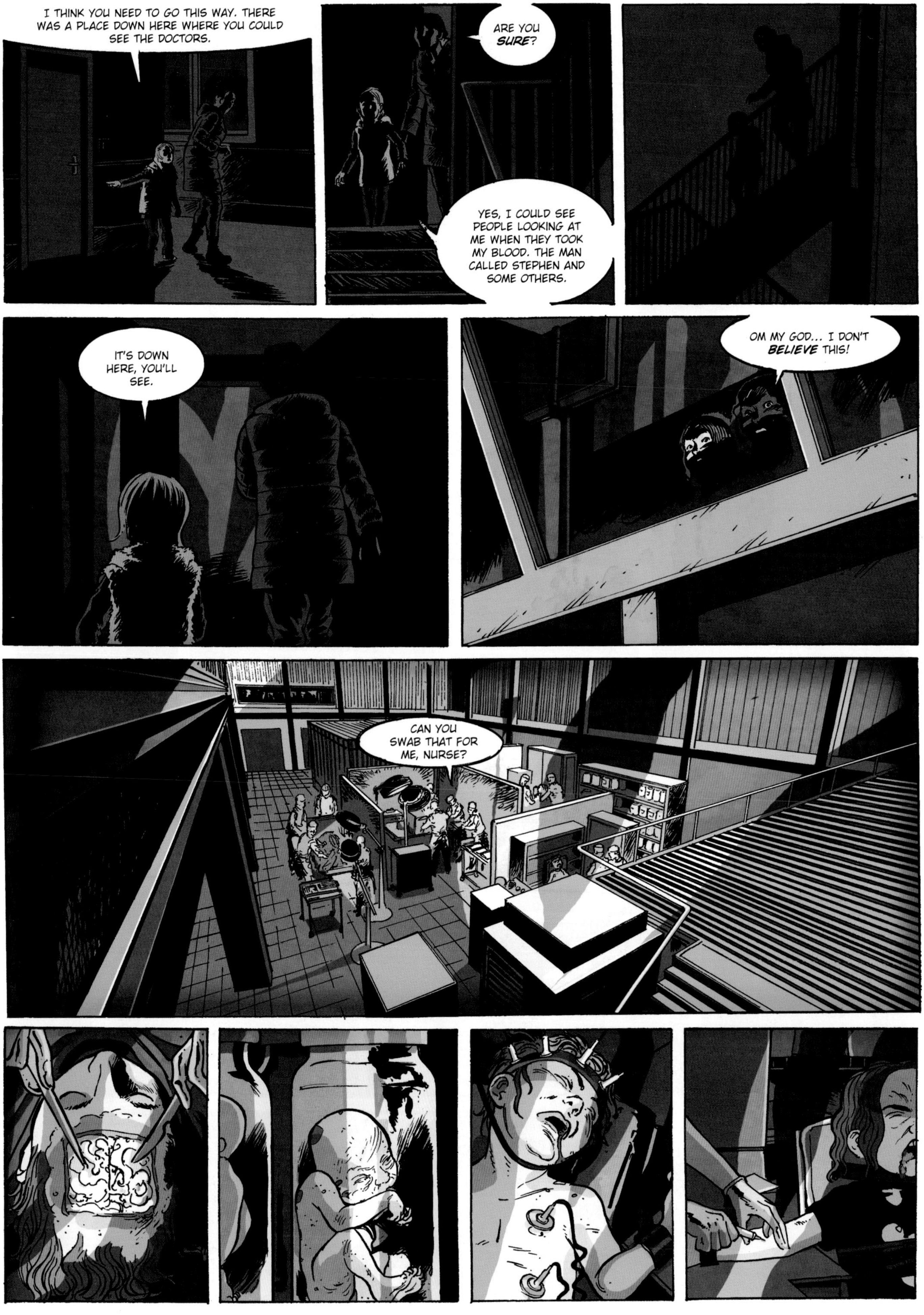

I THINK YOU NEED TO GO THIS WAY. THERE WAS A PLACE DOWN HERE WHERE YOU COULD SEE THE DOCTORS.
ARE YOU SURE?
YES, I COULD SEE PEOPLE LOOKING AT ME WHEN THEY TOOK MY BLOOD. THE MAN CALLED STEPHEN AND SOME OTHERS.
IT'S DOWN HERE, YOU'LL SEE.
OM MY GOD... I DON'T BELIEVE THIS!
CAN YOU SWAB THAT FOR ME, NURSE?

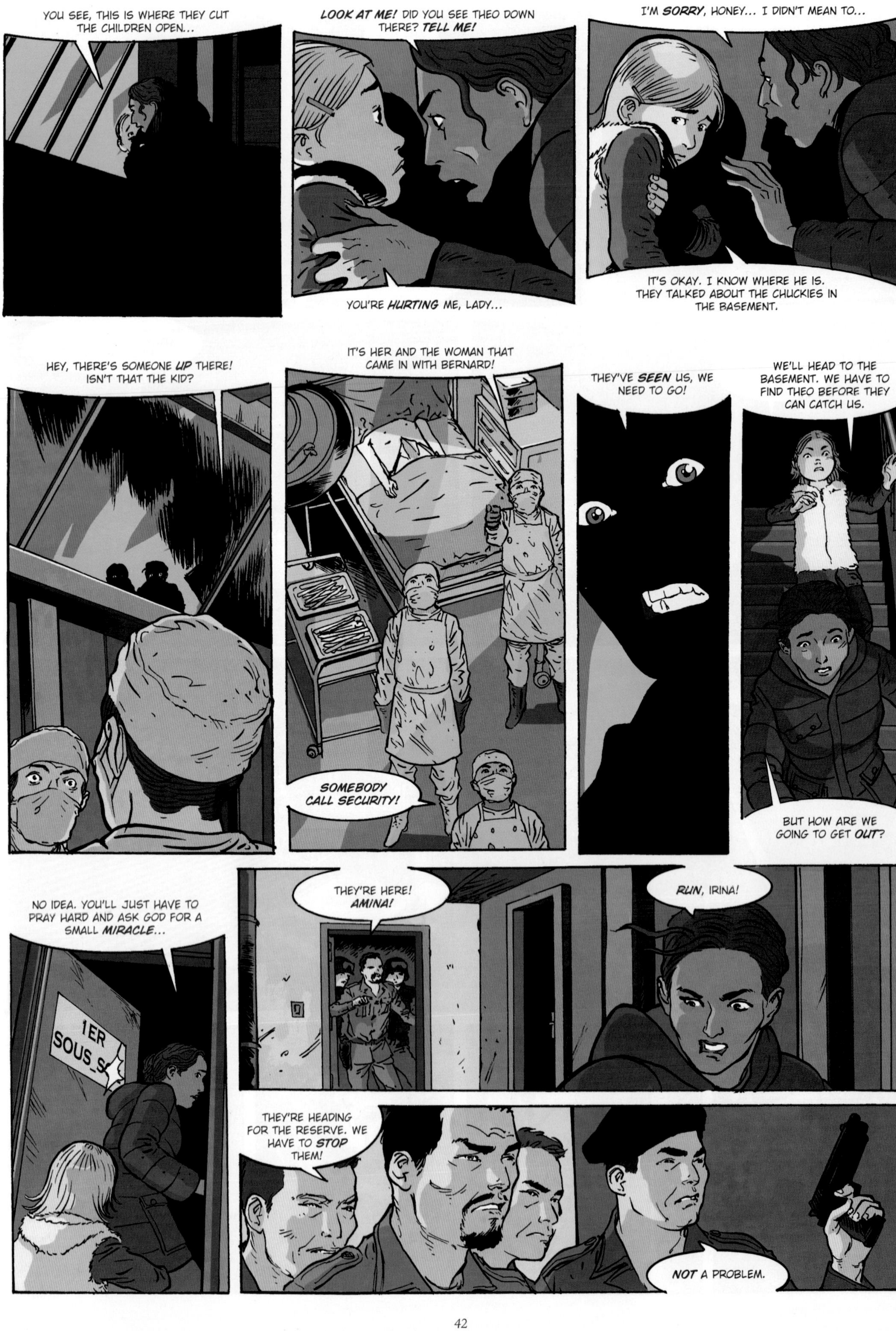

YOU SEE, THIS IS WHERE THEY CUT THE CHILDREN OPEN...
LOOK AT ME! DID YOU SEE THEO DOWN THERE? TELL ME!
YOU'RE HURTING ME, LADY...
I'M SORRY, HONEY... I DIDN'T MEAN TO...
IT'S OKAY. I KNOW WHERE HE IS. THEY TALKED ABOUT THE CHUCKIES IN THE BASEMENT.
HEY, THERE'S SOMEONE UP THERE! ISN'T THAT THE KID?
IT'S HER AND THE WOMAN THAT CAME IN WITH BERNARD!
SOMEBODY CALL SECURITY!
THEY'VE SEEN US, WE NEED TO GO!
WE'LL HEAD TO THE BASEMENT. WE HAVE TO FIND THEO BEFORE THEY CAN CATCH US.
BUT HOW ARE WE GOING TO GET OUT?
NO IDEA. YOU'LL JUST HAVE TO PRAY HARD AND ASK GOD FOR A SMALL MIRACLE...
1ER SOUS_S
THEY'RE HERE! AMINA!
RUN, IRINA!
THEY'RE HEADING FOR THE RESERVE. WE HAVE TO STOP THEM!
NOT A PROBLEM.

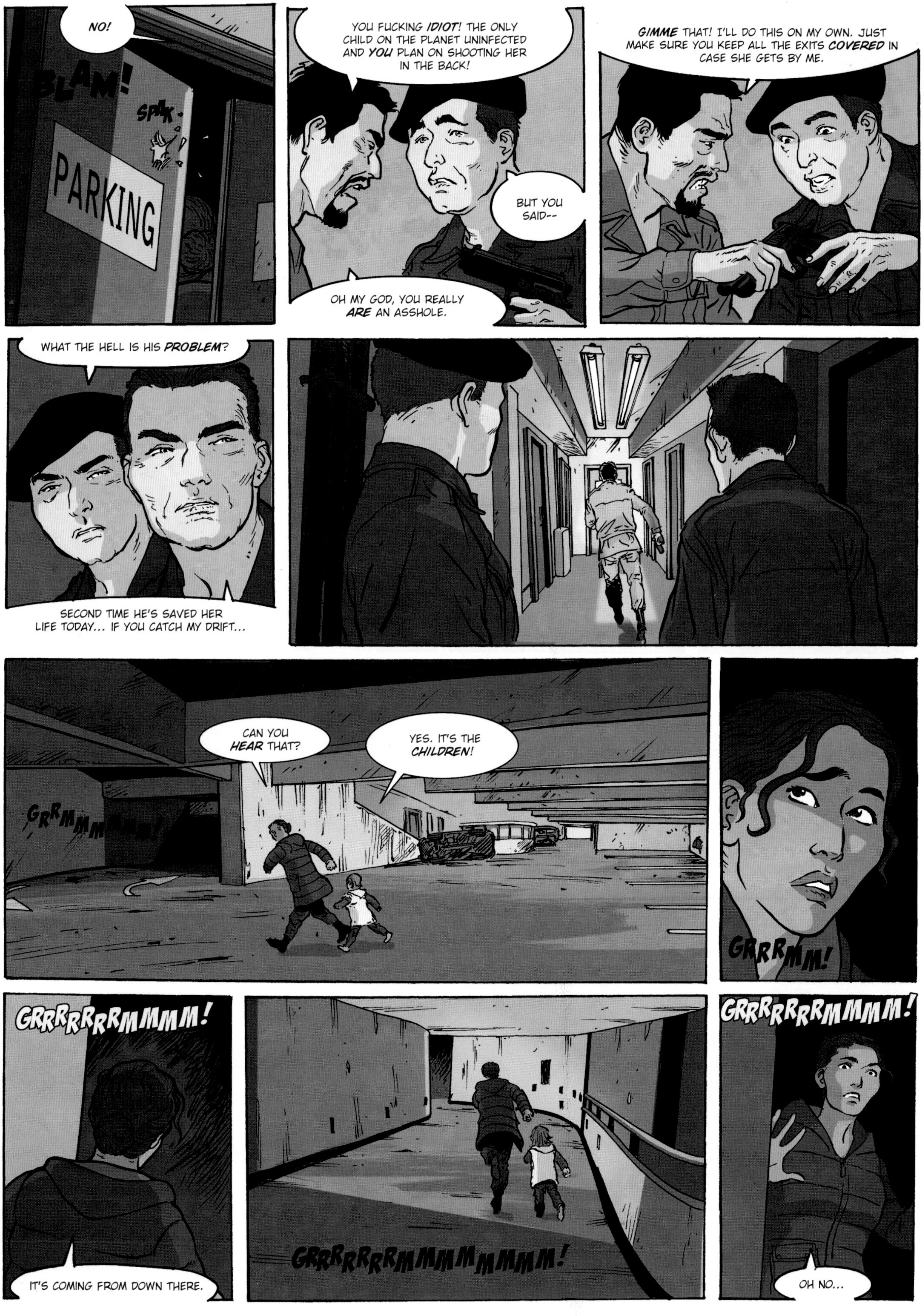
NO!
BLAM!
SPAK
PARKING
YOU FUCKING IDIOT! THE ONLY CHILD ON THE PLANET UNINFECTED AND YOU PLAN ON SHOOTING HER IN THE BACK!
BUT YOU SAID--
OH MY GOD, YOU REALLY ARE AN ASSHOLE.
GIMME THAT! I'LL DO THIS ON MY OWN. JUST MAKE SURE YOU KEEP ALL THE EXITS COVERED IN CASE SHE GETS BY ME.
WHAT THE HELL IS HIS PROBLEM?
SECOND TIME HE'S SAVED HER LIFE TODAY... IF YOU CATCH MY DRIFT...
CAN YOU HEAR THAT?
YES. IT'S THE CHILDREN!
GRRMMMMM!
GRRRMM!
GRRRRRRRMMMM!
IT'S COMING FROM DOWN THERE.
GRRRRRRRMMMMMMMMM!
GRRRRRRRMMMM!
OH NO...

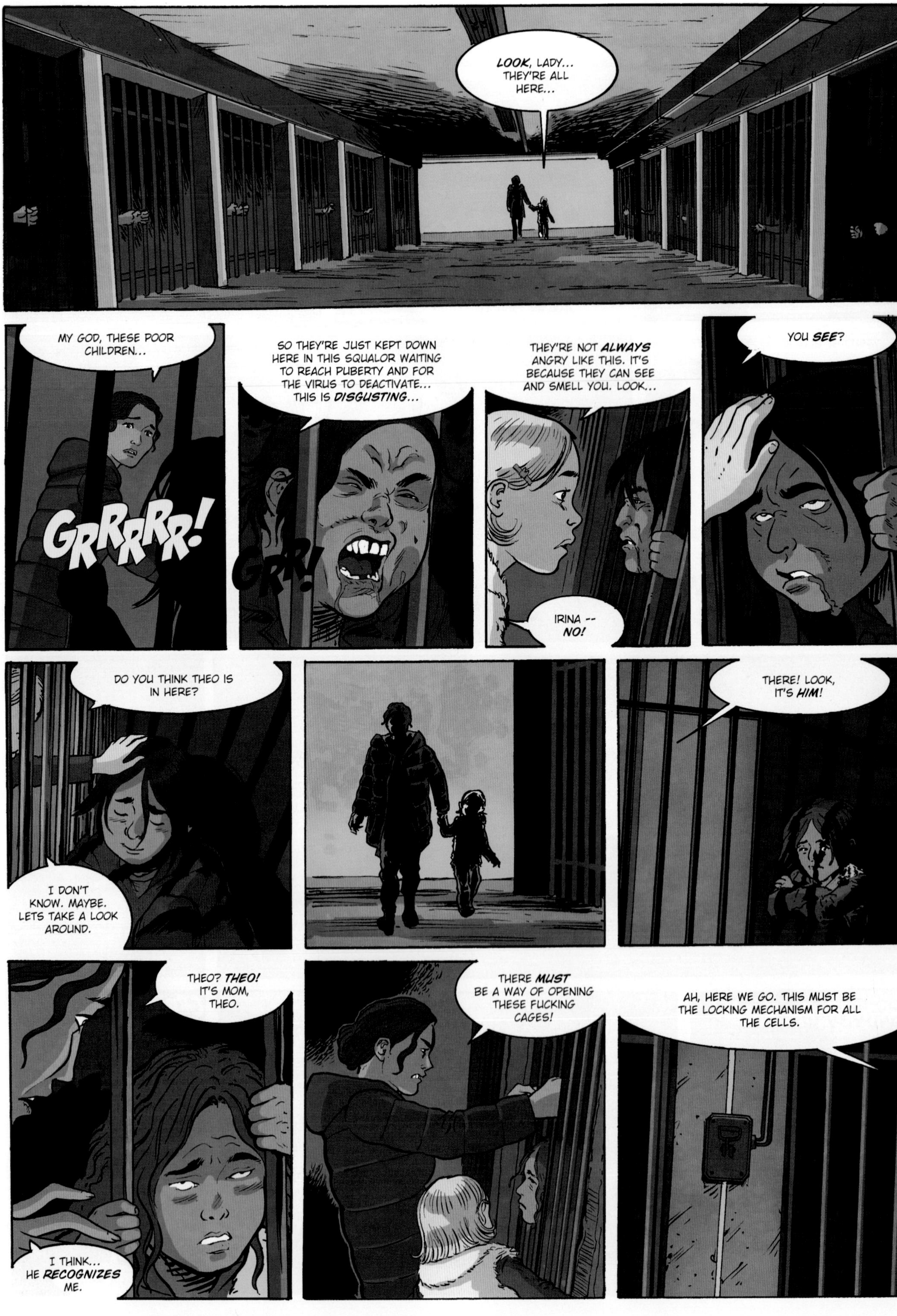

LOOK, LADY... THEY'RE ALL HERE...
MY GOD, THESE POOR CHILDREN...
GRRRRR!
SO THEY'RE JUST KEPT DOWN HERE IN THIS SQUALOR WAITING TO REACH PUBERTY AND FOR THE VIRUS TO DEACTIVATE... THIS IS DISGUSTING...
GRR!
THEY'RE NOT ALWAYS ANGRY LIKE THIS. IT'S BECAUSE THEY CAN SEE AND SMELL YOU. LOOK...
IRINA -- NO!
YOU SEE?
DO YOU THINK THEO IS IN HERE?
I DON'T KNOW. MAYBE. LETS TAKE A LOOK AROUND.
THERE! LOOK, IT'S HIM!
THEO? THEO! IT'S MOM, THEO.
I THINK... HE RECOGNIZES ME.
THERE MUST BE A WAY OF OPENING THESE FUCKING CAGES!
AH, HERE WE GO. THIS MUST BE THE LOCKING MECHANISM FOR ALL THE CELLS.

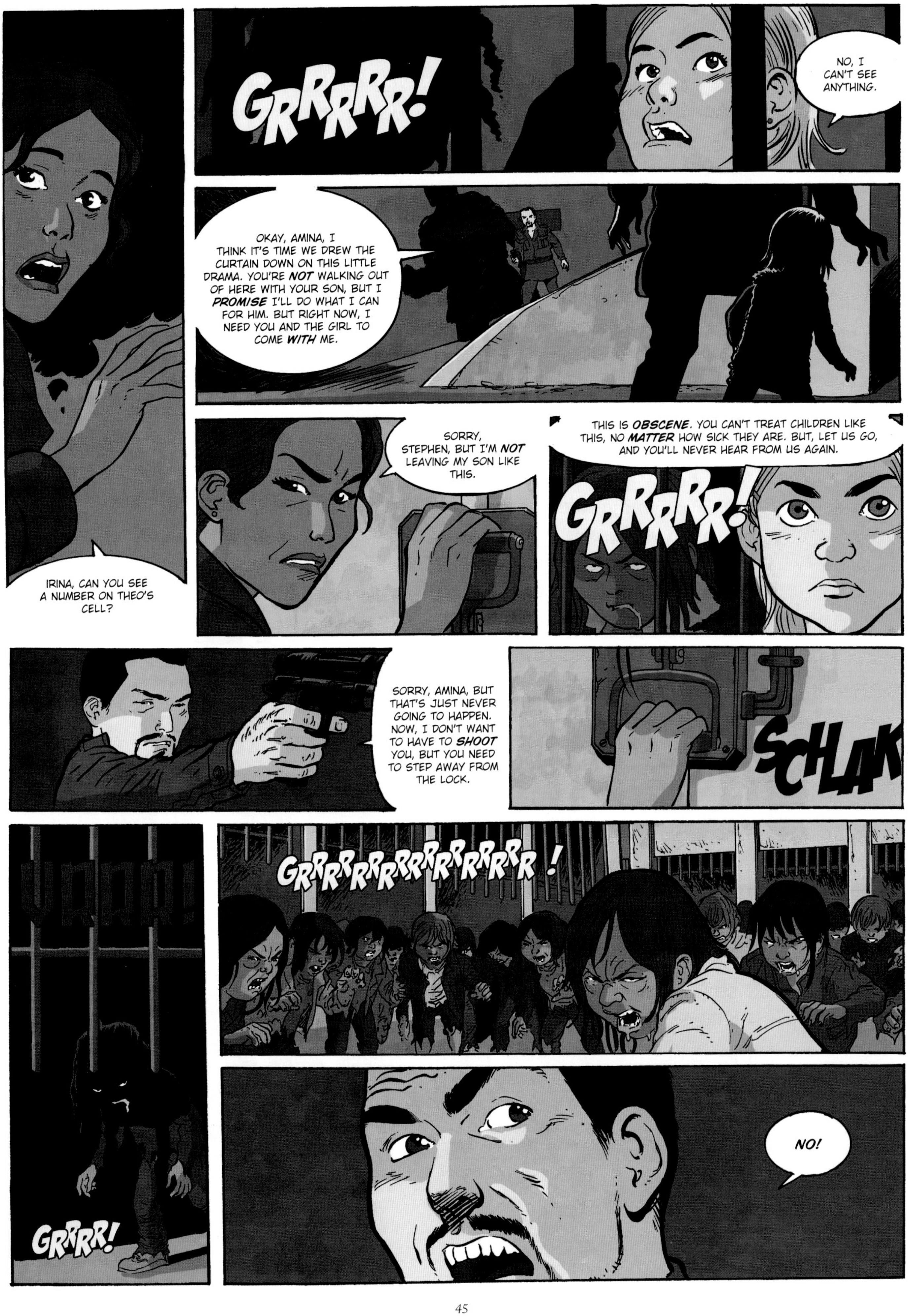
IRINA, CAN YOU SEE A NUMBER ON THEO'S CELL?
GRRRRR!
NO, I CAN'T SEE ANYTHING.
OKAY, AMINA, I THINK IT'S TIME WE DREW THE CURTAIN DOWN ON THIS LITTLE DRAMA. YOU'RE **NOT** WALKING OUT OF HERE WITH YOUR SON, BUT I **PROMISE** I'LL DO WHAT I CAN FOR HIM. BUT RIGHT NOW, I NEED YOU AND THE GIRL TO COME **WITH** ME.
SORRY, STEPHEN, BUT I'M **NOT** LEAVING MY SON LIKE THIS.
THIS IS **OBSCENE**. YOU CAN'T TREAT CHILDREN LIKE THIS, NO **MATTER** HOW SICK THEY ARE. BUT, LET US GO, AND YOU'LL NEVER HEAR FROM US AGAIN.
GRRRRR!
SORRY, AMINA, BUT THAT'S JUST NEVER GOING TO HAPPEN. NOW, I DON'T WANT TO HAVE TO **SHOOT** YOU, BUT YOU NEED TO STEP AWAY FROM THE LOCK.
SCHLAK
GRRRR!
GRRRRRRRRRRRRRR !
NO!

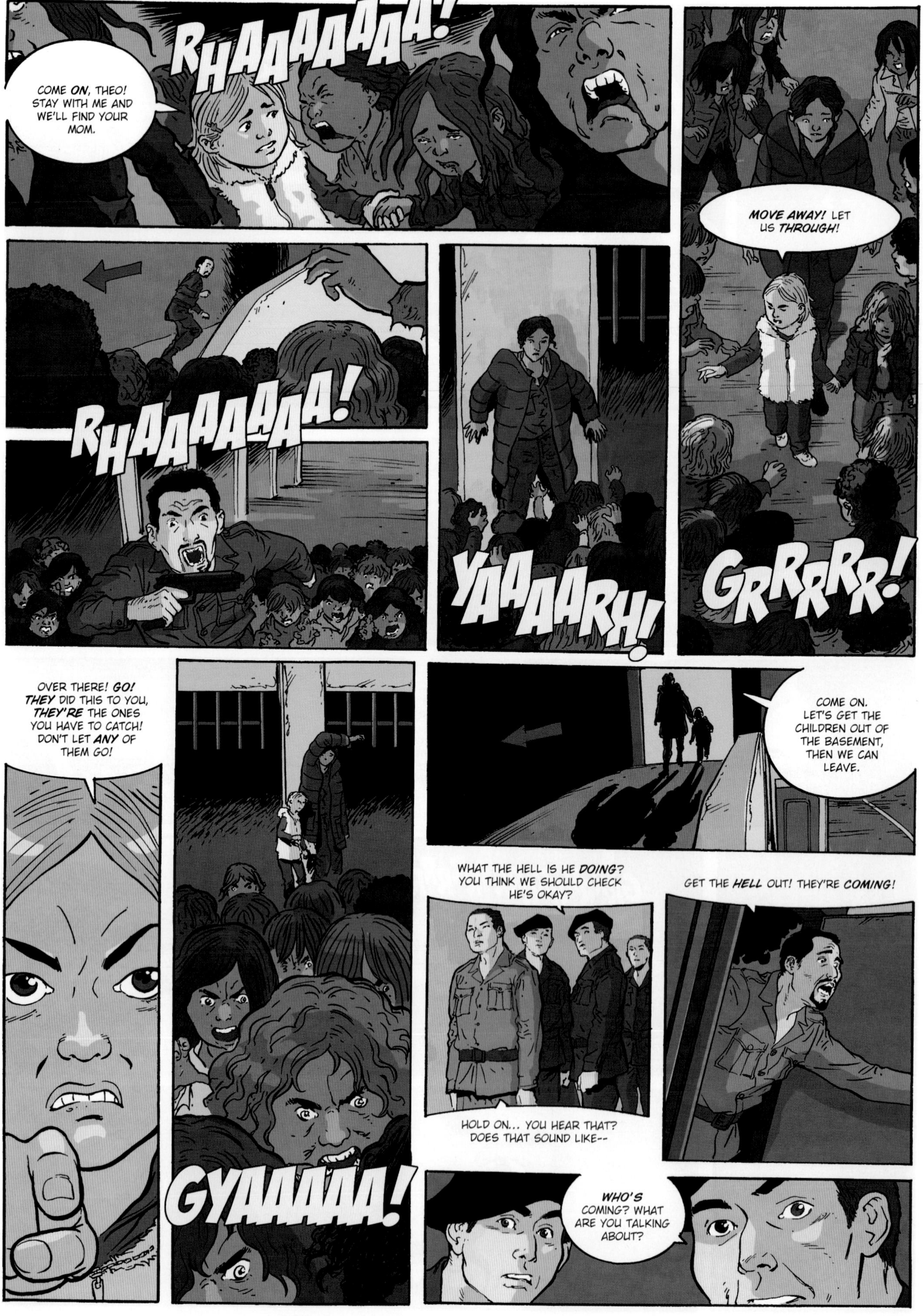
RHAAAAAAA!
COME ON, THEO! STAY WITH ME AND WE'LL FIND YOUR MOM.
MOVE AWAY! LET US THROUGH!
RHAAAAAAA!
YAAAARH!
GRRRRR!
OVER THERE! GO! THEY DID THIS TO YOU, THEY'RE THE ONES YOU HAVE TO CATCH! DON'T LET ANY OF THEM GO!
GYAAAAA!
COME ON. LET'S GET THE CHILDREN OUT OF THE BASEMENT, THEN WE CAN LEAVE.
WHAT THE HELL IS HE DOING? YOU THINK WE SHOULD CHECK HE'S OKAY?
HOLD ON... YOU HEAR THAT? DOES THAT SOUND LIKE--
GET THE HELL OUT! THEY'RE COMING!
WHO'S COMING? WHAT ARE YOU TALKING ABOUT?

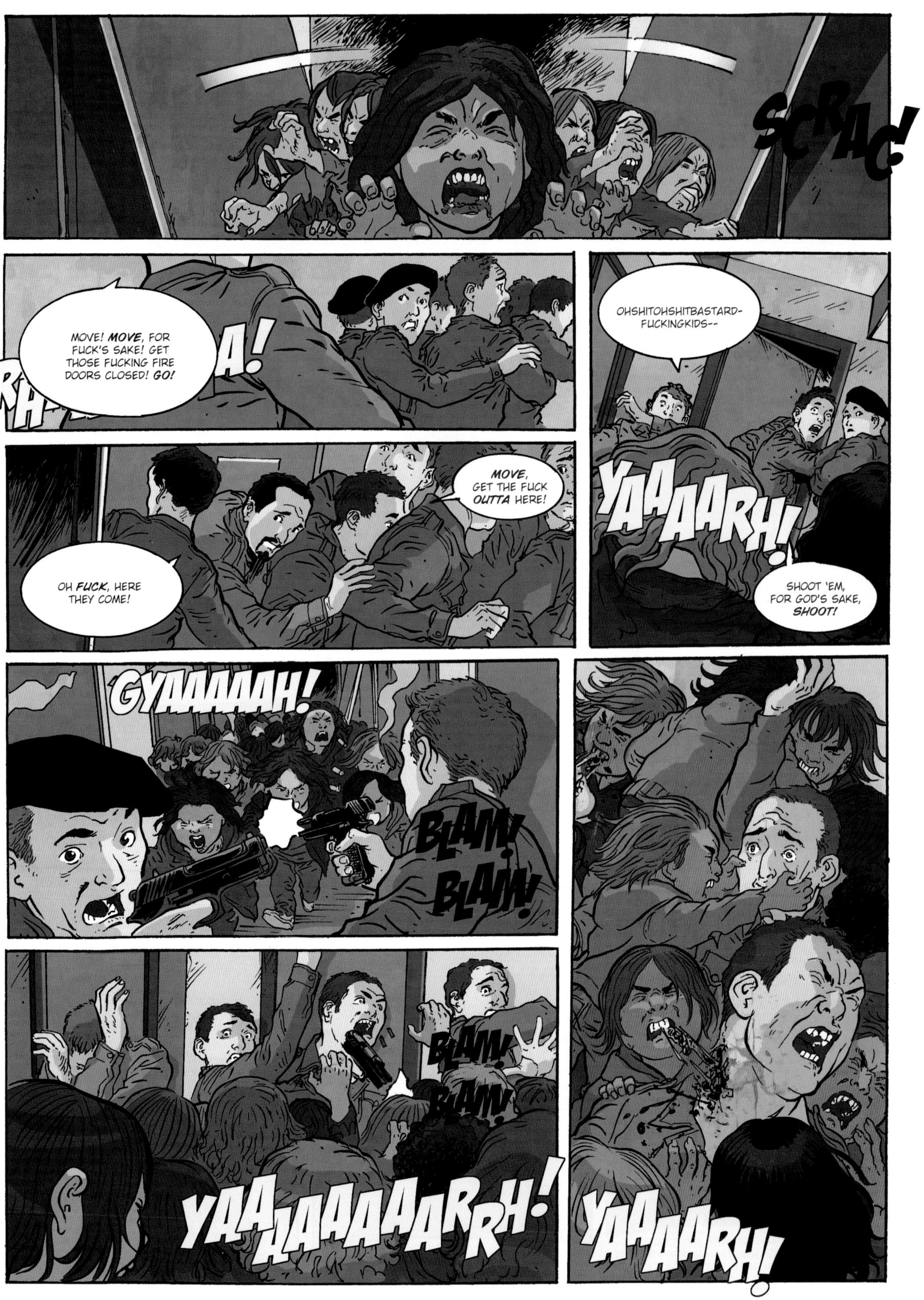
SCRAC!
RHA... A!
MOVE! MOVE, FOR FUCK'S SAKE! GET THOSE FUCKING FIRE DOORS CLOSED! GO!
OHSHITOHSHITBASTARD-FUCKINGKIDS--
MOVE, GET THE FUCK OUTTA HERE!
OH FUCK, HERE THEY COME!
YAAAARH!
SHOOT 'EM, FOR GOD'S SAKE, SHOOT!
GYAAAAAH!
BLAM! BLAM!
BLAM! BLAM!
YAAAAAAAARRH!
YAAAARH!

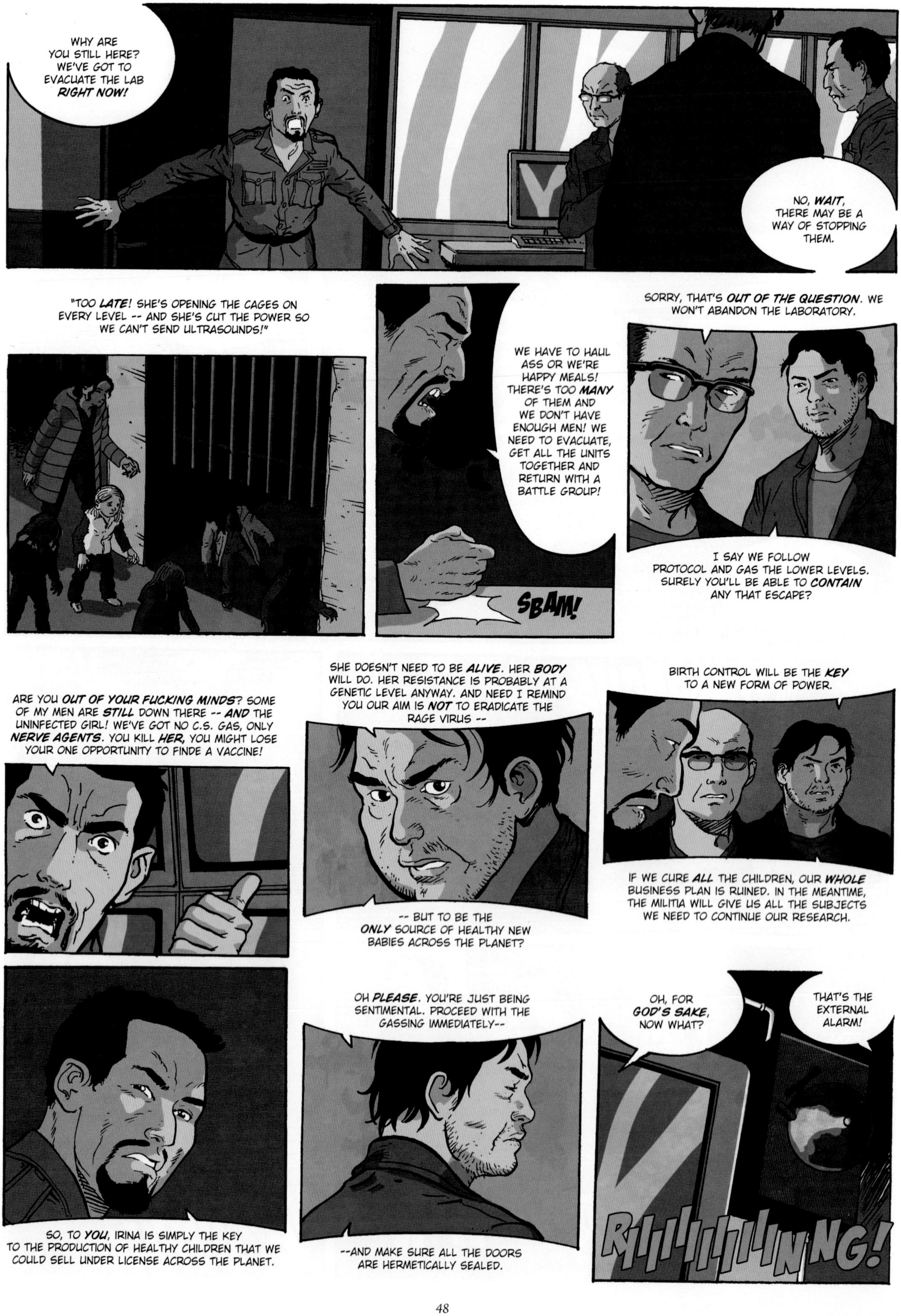
WHY ARE YOU STILL HERE? WE'VE GOT TO EVACUATE THE LAB RIGHT NOW!
NO, WAIT, THERE MAY BE A WAY OF STOPPING THEM.
"TOO LATE! SHE'S OPENING THE CAGES ON EVERY LEVEL -- AND SHE'S CUT THE POWER SO WE CAN'T SEND ULTRASOUNDS!"
WE HAVE TO HAUL ASS OR WE'RE HAPPY MEALS! THERE'S TOO MANY OF THEM AND WE DON'T HAVE ENOUGH MEN! WE NEED TO EVACUATE, GET ALL THE UNITS TOGETHER AND RETURN WITH A BATTLE GROUP!
SBAM!
SORRY, THAT'S OUT OF THE QUESTION. WE WON'T ABANDON THE LABORATORY.
I SAY WE FOLLOW PROTOCOL AND GAS THE LOWER LEVELS. SURELY YOU'LL BE ABLE TO CONTAIN ANY THAT ESCAPE?
ARE YOU OUT OF YOUR FUCKING MINDS? SOME OF MY MEN ARE STILL DOWN THERE -- AND THE UNINFECTED GIRL! WE'VE GOT NO C.S. GAS, ONLY NERVE AGENTS. YOU KILL HER, YOU MIGHT LOSE YOUR ONE OPPORTUNITY TO FINDE A VACCINE!
SHE DOESN'T NEED TO BE ALIVE. HER BODY WILL DO. HER RESISTANCE IS PROBABLY AT A GENETIC LEVEL ANYWAY. AND NEED I REMIND YOU OUR AIM IS NOT TO ERADICATE THE RAGE VIRUS --
-- BUT TO BE THE ONLY SOURCE OF HEALTHY NEW BABIES ACROSS THE PLANET?
BIRTH CONTROL WILL BE THE KEY TO A NEW FORM OF POWER.
IF WE CURE ALL THE CHILDREN, OUR WHOLE BUSINESS PLAN IS RUINED. IN THE MEANTIME, THE MILITIA WILL GIVE US ALL THE SUBJECTS WE NEED TO CONTINUE OUR RESEARCH.
SO, TO YOU, IRINA IS SIMPLY THE KEY TO THE PRODUCTION OF HEALTHY CHILDREN THAT WE COULD SELL UNDER LICENSE ACROSS THE PLANET.
OH PLEASE. YOU'RE JUST BEING SENTIMENTAL. PROCEED WITH THE GASSING IMMEDIATELY--
--AND MAKE SURE ALL THE DOORS ARE HERMETICALLY SEALED.
OH, FOR GOD'S SAKE, NOW WHAT?
THAT'S THE EXTERNAL ALARM!
RIIIIIIIIIIINNG!

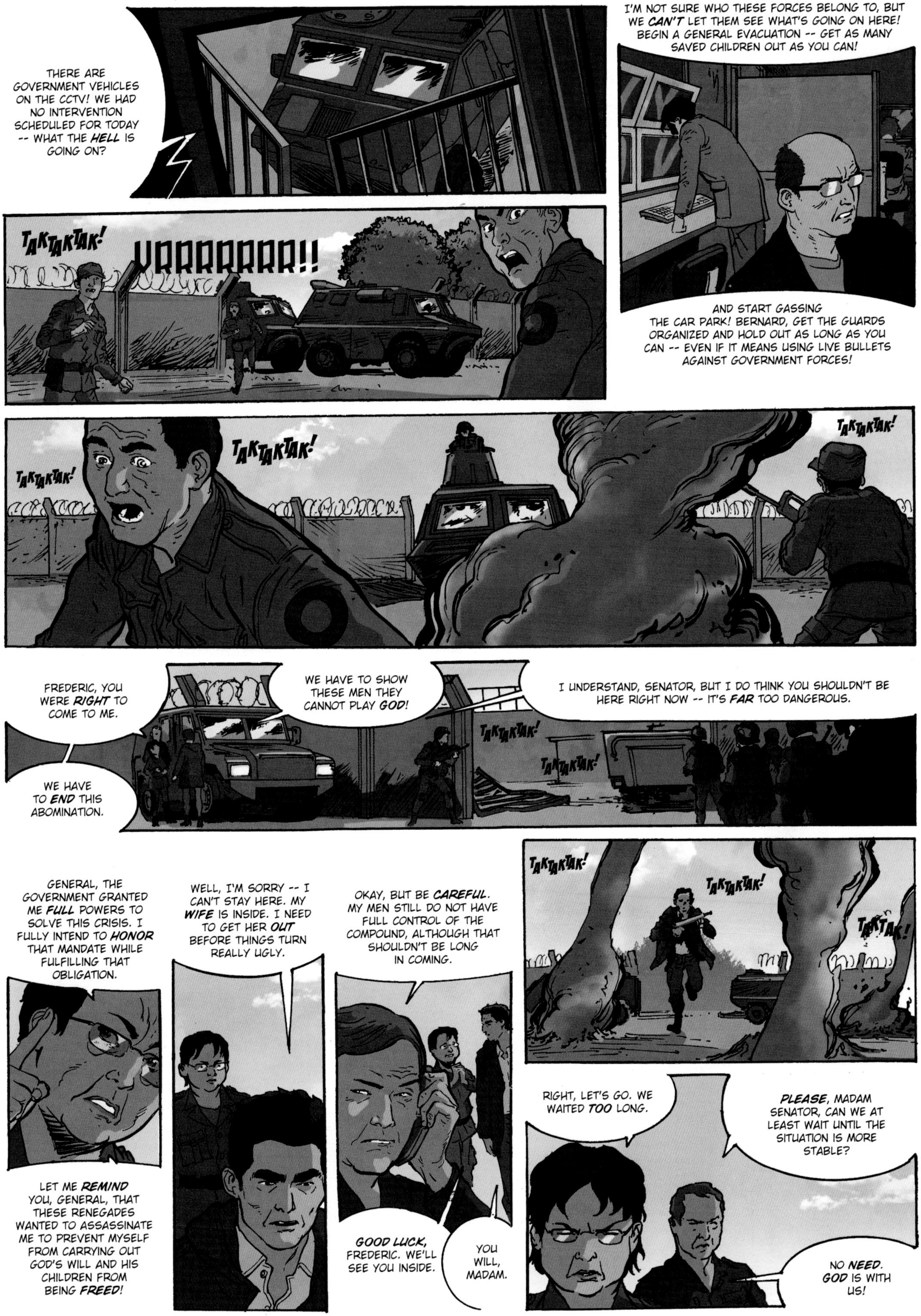
THERE ARE GOVERNMENT VEHICLES ON THE CCTV! WE HAD NO INTERVENTION SCHEDULED FOR TODAY -- WHAT THE HELL IS GOING ON?
I'M NOT SURE WHO THESE FORCES BELONG TO, BUT WE CAN'T LET THEM SEE WHAT'S GOING ON HERE! BEGIN A GENERAL EVACUATION -- GET AS MANY SAVED CHILDREN OUT AS YOU CAN!
TAKTAKTAK!
VRRRRRRR!!
AND START GASSING THE CAR PARK! BERNARD, GET THE GUARDS ORGANIZED AND HOLD OUT AS LONG AS YOU CAN -- EVEN IF IT MEANS USING LIVE BULLETS AGAINST GOVERNMENT FORCES!
TAKTAKTAK!
TAKTAKTAK!
TAKTAKTAK!
FREDERIC, YOU WERE RIGHT TO COME TO ME.
WE HAVE TO END THIS ABOMINATION.
WE HAVE TO SHOW THESE MEN THEY CANNOT PLAY GOD!
I UNDERSTAND, SENATOR, BUT I DO THINK YOU SHOULDN'T BE HERE RIGHT NOW -- IT'S FAR TOO DANGEROUS.
TAKTAKTAK!
TAKTAKTAK!
GENERAL, THE GOVERNMENT GRANTED ME FULL POWERS TO SOLVE THIS CRISIS. I FULLY INTEND TO HONOR THAT MANDATE WHILE FULFILLING THAT OBLIGATION.
LET ME REMIND YOU, GENERAL, THAT THESE RENEGADES WANTED TO ASSASSINATE ME TO PREVENT MYSELF FROM CARRYING OUT GOD'S WILL AND HIS CHILDREN FROM BEING FREED!
WELL, I'M SORRY -- I CAN'T STAY HERE. MY WIFE IS INSIDE. I NEED TO GET HER OUT BEFORE THINGS TURN REALLY UGLY.
OKAY, BUT BE CAREFUL. MY MEN STILL DO NOT HAVE FULL CONTROL OF THE COMPOUND, ALTHOUGH THAT SHOULDN'T BE LONG IN COMING.
GOOD LUCK, FREDERIC. WE'LL SEE YOU INSIDE.
YOU WILL, MADAM.
TAKTAKTAK!
TAKTAKTAK!
TAKTAK!
RIGHT, LET'S GO. WE WAITED TOO LONG.
PLEASE, MADAM SENATOR, CAN WE AT LEAST WAIT UNTIL THE SITUATION IS MORE STABLE?
NO NEED. GOD IS WITH US!

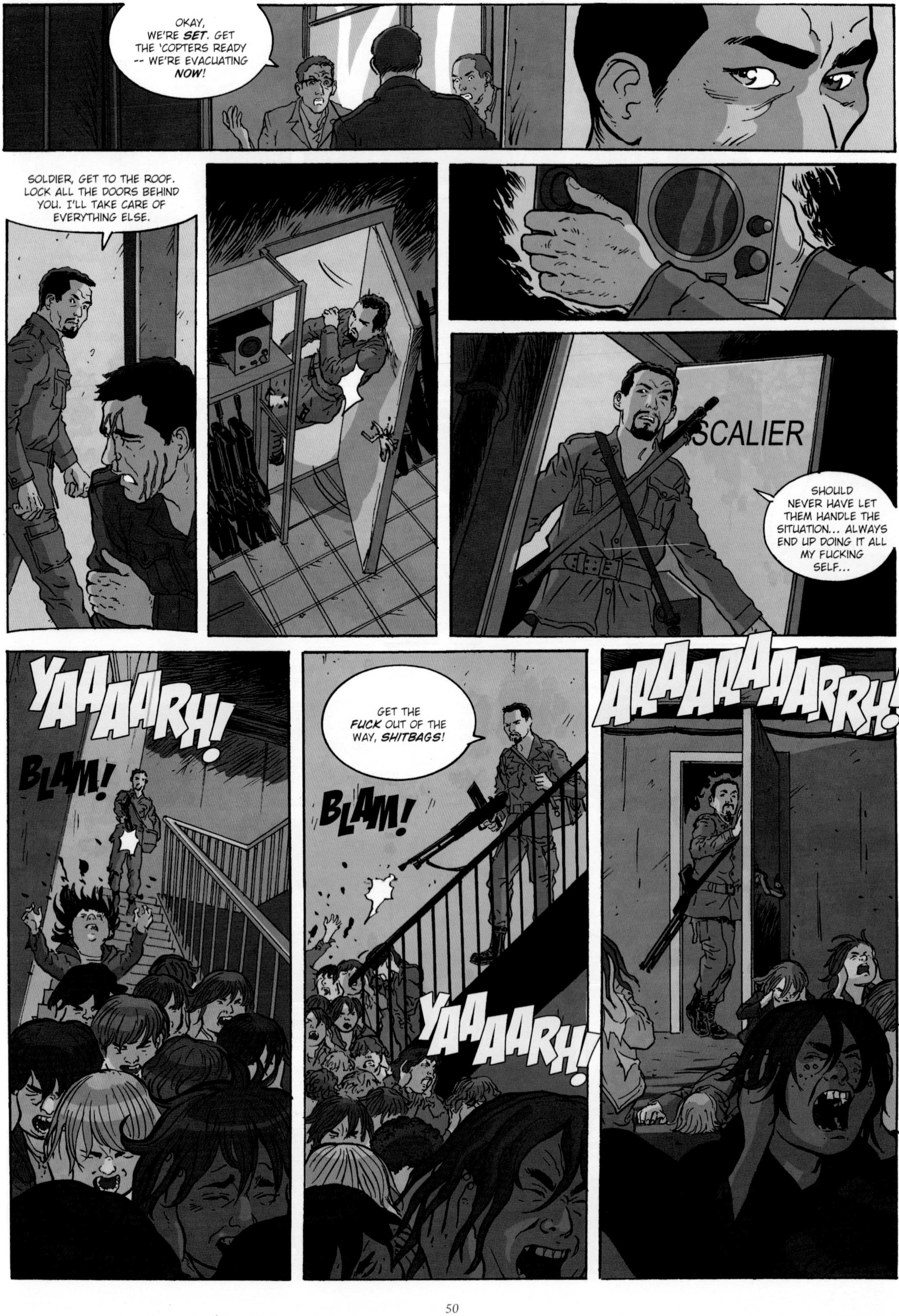

OKAY, WE'RE SET. GET THE 'COPTERS READY -- WE'RE EVACUATING NOW!
SOLDIER, GET TO THE ROOF. LOCK ALL THE DOORS BEHIND YOU. I'LL TAKE CARE OF EVERYTHING ELSE.
SCALIER
SHOULD NEVER HAVE LET THEM HANDLE THE SITUATION... ALWAYS END UP DOING IT ALL MY FUCKING SELF...
YAAAARH!
BLAM!
GET THE FUCK OUT OF THE WAY, SHITBAGS!
BLAM!
YAAAARH!
ARAAARAAAARRH!

YAAAAAAAAAAAARRH!!

WHHIIIHJ!

AMINA! HOLD UP, I NEED TO TALK TO YOU.

AHHHHHH! IT *HURTS*!

IRINA! WHAT'S HAPPENING?! IS IT--? OH YOU BASTARD AND YOUR FUCKING ULTRASOUND!

WHHIIIHJ!

IRINA -- LISTEN, WE HAVE TO HEAD UP AND GET *OUT* OF HERE!

AMINA, *NO*! THERE'S A *WAR* BEING FOUGHT UP THERE -- YOU HAVE TO STAY! I CAN *PROTECT* YOU!

GODDAMN *IDIOTS*! THE GAS IS JUST GOING TO DRIVE THE CHUCKIES UP INTO THE FIGHTING!

SSHHH!

ALL OF YOU, STAY WHERE YOU ARE! I'M CAPTAIN CHIRAZI! THIS LAB IS NOW UNDER THE CONTROL OF LOYALIST FORCES!

WAIT, WE HAVE TO GET *OUT* OF HERE! THERE ARE PACKS OF CHUCKIES ON THEIR WAY UP!

SHUT UP! YOU'RE ALL GOING TO BE CHARGED WITH TREASON FOR COLLUDING WITH HEROD'S MILITIA. YOU'RE LUCKY WE DON'T JUST SHOOT YOU NOW.

YES, GENERAL, LAB IS SECURE.

WE HAVE THE SITUATION UNDER CONTROL, YOU CAN COME IN.

OKAY, CAPTAIN, I'LL TAKE IT FROM HERE.

SO *THIS* IS THE RENEGADES' *LAIR*?!

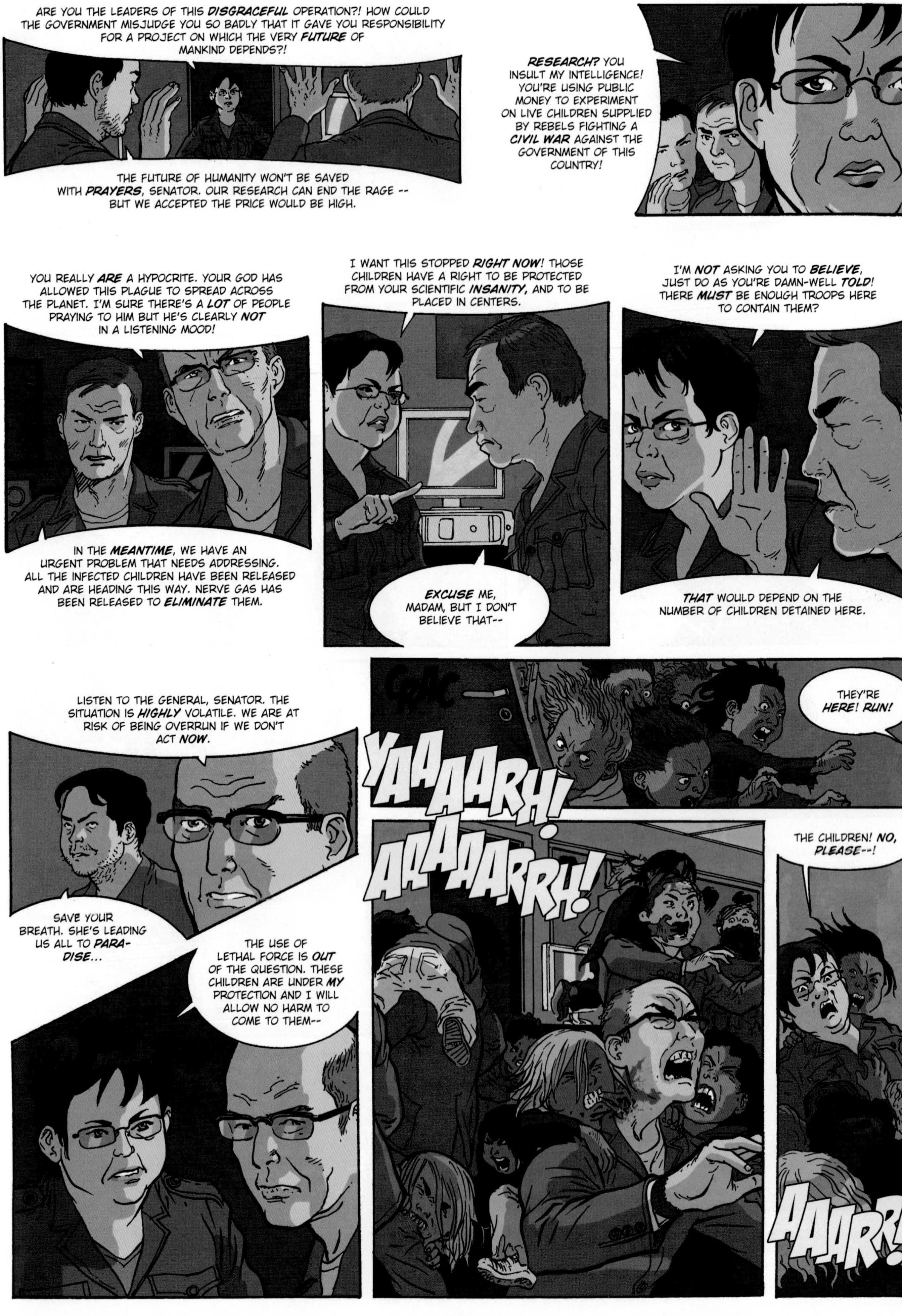
ARE YOU THE LEADERS OF THIS DISGRACEFUL OPERATION?! HOW COULD THE GOVERNMENT MISJUDGE YOU SO BADLY THAT IT GAVE YOU RESPONSIBILITY FOR A PROJECT ON WHICH THE VERY FUTURE OF MANKIND DEPENDS?!
THE FUTURE OF HUMANITY WON'T BE SAVED WITH PRAYERS, SENATOR. OUR RESEARCH CAN END THE RAGE -- BUT WE ACCEPTED THE PRICE WOULD BE HIGH.
RESEARCH? YOU INSULT MY INTELLIGENCE! YOU'RE USING PUBLIC MONEY TO EXPERIMENT ON LIVE CHILDREN SUPPLIED BY REBELS FIGHTING A CIVIL WAR AGAINST THE GOVERNMENT OF THIS COUNTRY!
YOU REALLY ARE A HYPOCRITE. YOUR GOD HAS ALLOWED THIS PLAGUE TO SPREAD ACROSS THE PLANET. I'M SURE THERE'S A LOT OF PEOPLE PRAYING TO HIM BUT HE'S CLEARLY NOT IN A LISTENING MOOD!
IN THE MEANTIME, WE HAVE AN URGENT PROBLEM THAT NEEDS ADDRESSING. ALL THE INFECTED CHILDREN HAVE BEEN RELEASED AND ARE HEADING THIS WAY. NERVE GAS HAS BEEN RELEASED TO ELIMINATE THEM.
I WANT THIS STOPPED RIGHT NOW! THOSE CHILDREN HAVE A RIGHT TO BE PROTECTED FROM YOUR SCIENTIFIC INSANITY, AND TO BE PLACED IN CENTERS.
EXCUSE ME, MADAM, BUT I DON'T BELIEVE THAT--
I'M NOT ASKING YOU TO BELIEVE, JUST DO AS YOU'RE DAMN-WELL TOLD! THERE MUST BE ENOUGH TROOPS HERE TO CONTAIN THEM?
THAT WOULD DEPEND ON THE NUMBER OF CHILDREN DETAINED HERE.
LISTEN TO THE GENERAL, SENATOR. THE SITUATION IS HIGHLY VOLATILE. WE ARE AT RISK OF BEING OVERRUN IF WE DON'T ACT NOW.
SAVE YOUR BREATH. SHE'S LEADING US ALL TO PARA-DISE...
THE USE OF LETHAL FORCE IS OUT OF THE QUESTION. THESE CHILDREN ARE UNDER MY PROTECTION AND I WILL ALLOW NO HARM TO COME TO THEM--
THEY'RE HERE! RUN!
YAAAARH!
AAAAAARRH!
THE CHILDREN! NO, PLEASE--!
AAARR!

AMINA! LISTEN TO ME! YOU **HAVE** TO TRUST ME! I'M THE **ONLY** ONE WHO CAN GET YOU OUT OF HERE!

WE'RE ALMOST THERE, KIDS, WE CAN **DO** THIS...

AMINA, **LISTEN** TO ME! GOVERNMENT FORCES ARE STORMING THE LAB, IT'S **DANGEROUS**!

NO! LEAVE US ALONE!

AHHHHHHH!

FRED!

SO **THIS** IS YOUR HUSBAND, CORRECT? A REGULAR FAMILY REUNION... BUT IT'S OVER, AMI. YOU'RE GOING TO COME WITH ME. I PROMISE I MEAN YOU NO HARM AND I'LL EXPLAIN EVERYTHING.

LET HER **GO**!

LET THE GIRL GO AND DROP YOUR WEAPON -- SLOWLY. BELIEVE ME, ONE WRONG MOVE AND I WILL BLOW YOUR BRAINS ALL OVER THIS ROOFTOP.

LISTEN, YOU'RE MAKING A **REALLY** BAD MISTAKE. IRINA CAN HELP US **ERADICATE** THE RAGE FROM THIS PLANET.

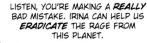

AND **THAT'S** WHY YOU WANTED TO **CUT HER UP**?! COME HERE, IRINA, QUICKLY NOW.

I **TOLD** YOU, DROP THE WEAPON.

BLAM!

FRED! NO, DON'T!

COME HERE, DARLING!

WHAT ARE YOU--

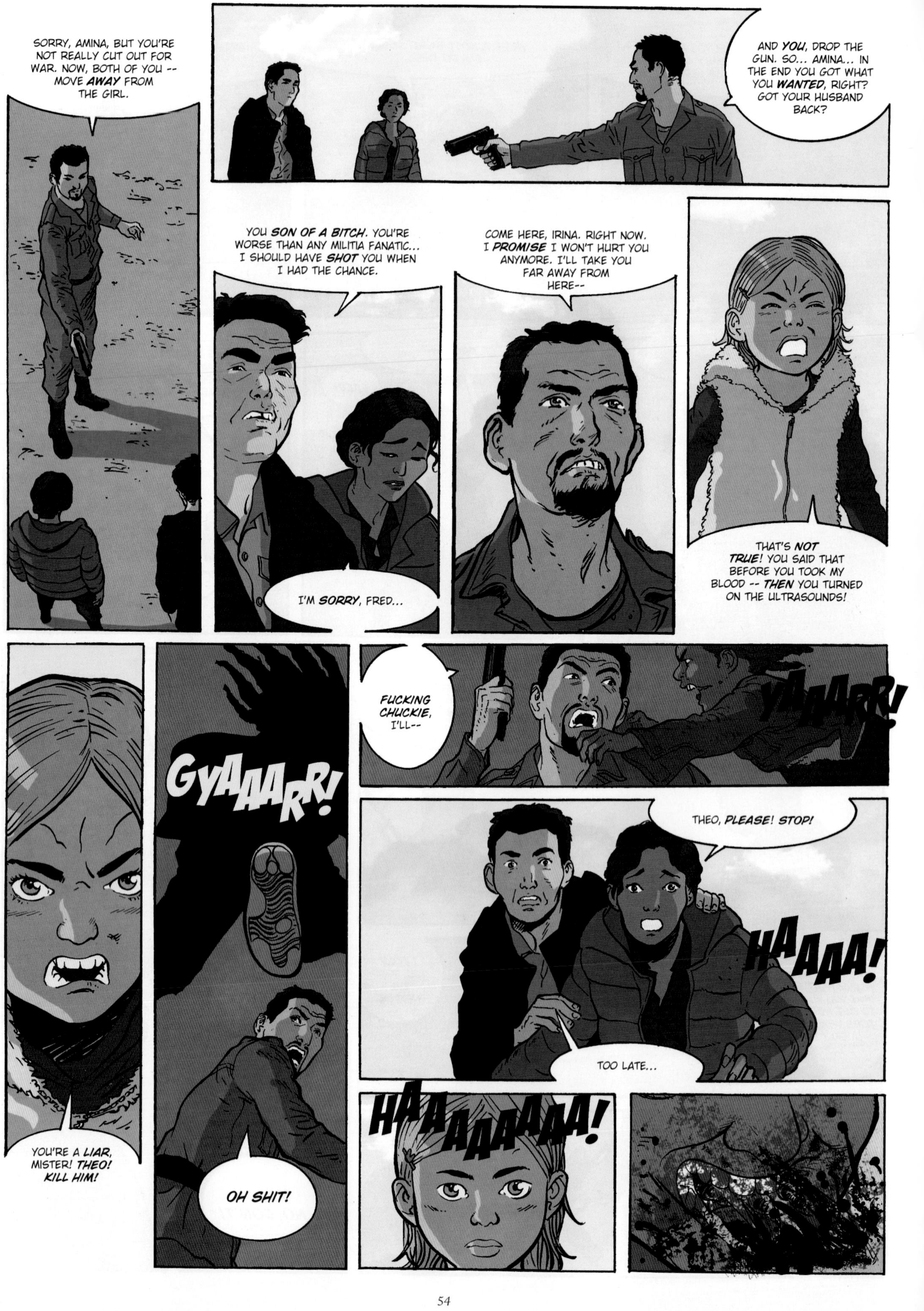
SORRY, AMINA, BUT YOU'RE NOT REALLY CUT OUT FOR WAR. NOW, BOTH OF YOU -- MOVE AWAY FROM THE GIRL.
AND YOU, DROP THE GUN. SO... AMINA... IN THE END YOU GOT WHAT YOU WANTED, RIGHT? GOT YOUR HUSBAND BACK?
YOU SON OF A BITCH. YOU'RE WORSE THAN ANY MILITIA FANATIC... I SHOULD HAVE SHOT YOU WHEN I HAD THE CHANCE.
I'M SORRY, FRED...
COME HERE, IRINA. RIGHT NOW. I PROMISE I WON'T HURT YOU ANYMORE. I'LL TAKE YOU FAR AWAY FROM HERE--
THAT'S NOT TRUE! YOU SAID THAT BEFORE YOU TOOK MY BLOOD -- THEN YOU TURNED ON THE ULTRASOUNDS!
YOU'RE A LIAR, MISTER! THEO! KILL HIM!
GYAAARR!
OH SHIT!
FUCKING CHUCKIE, I'LL--
YAAARR!
THEO, PLEASE! STOP!
HAAAA!
TOO LATE...
HAAAAAAAAA!

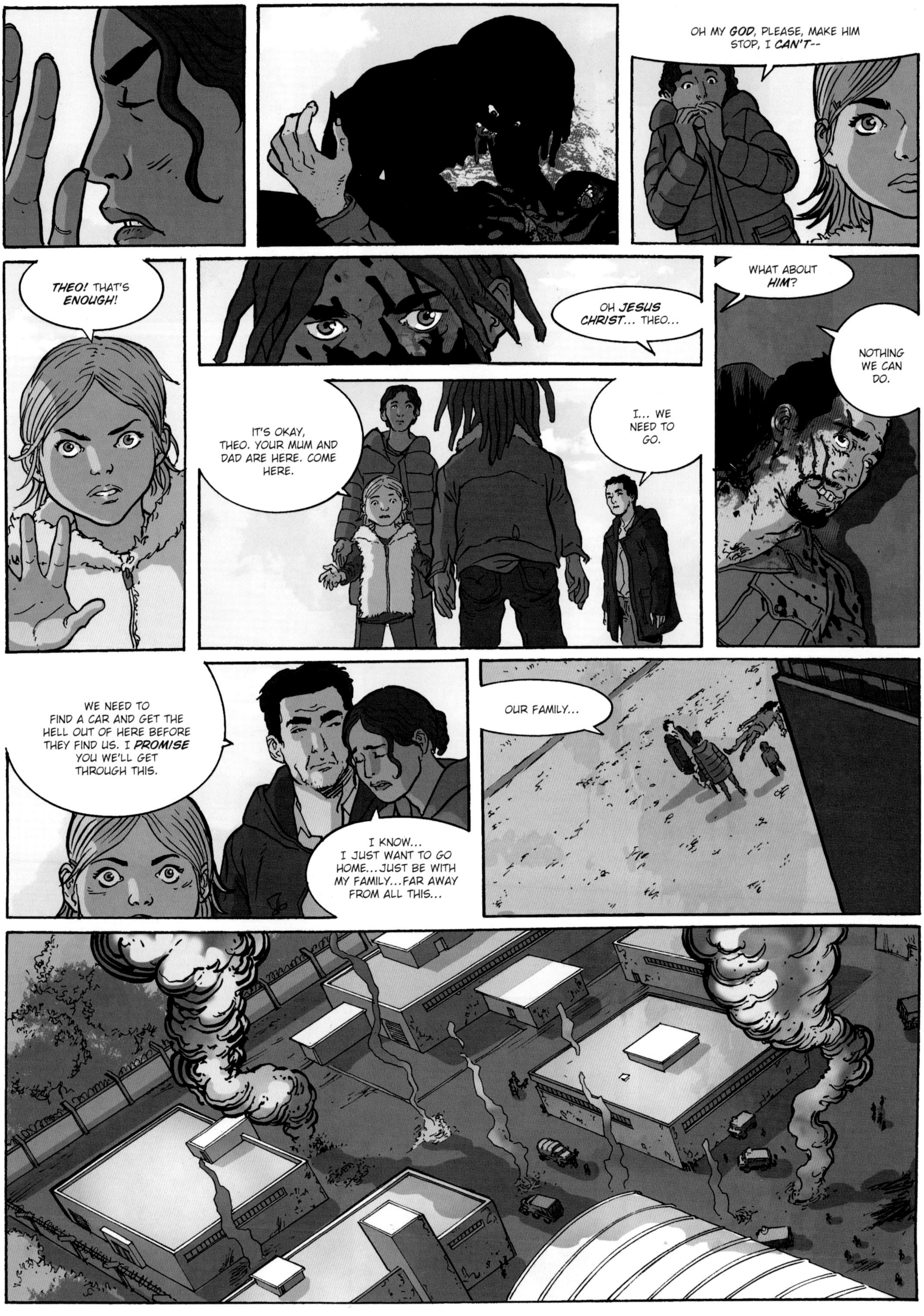
OH MY GOD, PLEASE, MAKE HIM STOP, I CAN'T--
THEO! THAT'S ENOUGH!
OH JESUS CHRIST... THEO...
WHAT ABOUT HIM?
NOTHING WE CAN DO.
IT'S OKAY, THEO. YOUR MUM AND DAD ARE HERE. COME HERE.
I... WE NEED TO GO.
WE NEED TO FIND A CAR AND GET THE HELL OUT OF HERE BEFORE THEY FIND US. I PROMISE YOU WE'LL GET THROUGH THIS.
I KNOW... I JUST WANT TO GO HOME... JUST BE WITH MY FAMILY...FAR AWAY FROM ALL THIS...
OUR FAMILY...

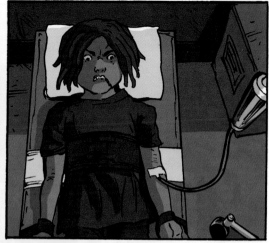

WE'RE LUCKY. THEO IS AB+

THIS IS GOOD, IRINA, BECAUSE IT MEANS HE CAN TAKE *ANYONE'S* BLOOD. THIS IS WHY I TOOK YOURS... I TOOK 200CCS FROM HER. HOPE IT'LL BE ENOUGH.

SO WILL MY BLOOD *CURE* HIM?

WE DON'T *KNOW*. YOUR IMMUNITY MAY COME FROM OTHER PARTS OF YOU.

I DON'T REALLY CARE. ALL THAT *MATTERS* IS THAT WE'RE TOGETHER...

WHETHER HE'S CURED OR NOT, WE CAN'T STAY HERE. THE LAB MASSACRE WILL HAVE REALLY LIT A FUSE UNDER THEM -- THEY'RE *BOUND* TO COME AFTER US.

I *KNOW*. I'VE GOT EVERYTHING PREPARED. WE'LL GO AS SOON AS THE TRANSFUSION IS COMPLETE.

WHERE ARE WE GOING?

THE END.